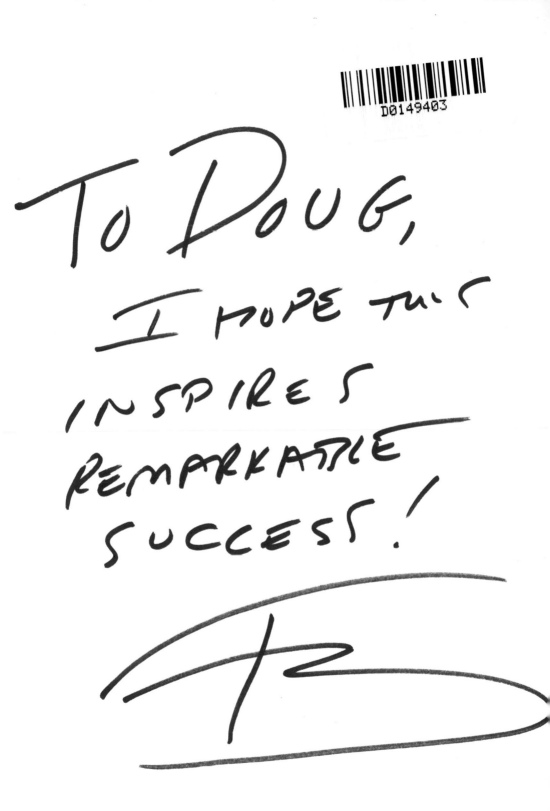

TO DOUG,

I HOPE THIS

INSPIRES

REMARKABLE

SUCCESS!

BECOMING
Remarkable

Creating a Dental Practice
Everyone Talks About

by Fred Joyal

CO-FOUNDER OF 1-800-DENTIST®

To Peter Stranger and Ken Berris,
who sparked and nurtured
my career in advertising,
from which my gloriously
abundant life has flowed.

CONTENTS

SECTION THREE: Creating the Remarkable Environment

SECTION FOUR: Building Your Remarkable Team

SECTION FIVE: Remarkable Actions

SECTION SIX: Practical Tools

SECTION SEVEN: Increasing Production

SECTION EIGHT: The Upward Spiral

INTRODUCTION

People talk.

But people have always talked, spreading the word about businesses they like or don't like—and why. The difference is when people talk *now*, they talk with their thumbs as much as their tongues. And what they write lives on, plus is searchable, sharable, likable, and, most important of all, *undeletable*. This is why you need to become remarkable.

Now when I say the word "remarkable," I mean it in two ways. The first is the more familiar use: being extraordinary or amazing. But I also mean it literally, as in: "worthy of being remarked about." I believe it has become imperative to be the kind of dentist, the kind of team member, the kind of practice that patients can't resist talking about.

I myself am not a dentist. But if I were, knowing what I know today, I would be a remarkable dentist. I'm not saying that to brag or out of hubris or conceit. I'm saying that it is the way of the future, the golden pathway to success on every level: monetarily, spiritually, and emotionally. I also believe that the alternative—being unremarkable—is the slow path to extinction.

We live in a world where reputation creates a permanent record. Almost like career criminals, we will all eventually end up with rap sheets a mile long. If we're not careful, we could very likely be remembered by our worst moments. In the age of Twitter®, Facebook®, and Yelp®, this has happened to a number of individuals, and it has negatively impacted many businesses. And the only way to effectively combat this is to, first, accept that it is not just the way of the future but the way of the present. Second, create an experience where not only do people *want* to talk positively about you, they can't resist doing it. That is the essence of what this book is designed to teach you.

Hopefully you've read my previous book, *Everything is Marketing*, because it serves as the foundation for this one. But if you haven't, I'm going to remind you of some key thoughts:

- First, dentistry is retail health care, which means the dentist and team need to get comfortable with and good at selling dentistry.
- Second, everything you do in your practice affects case acceptance—nothing is neutral. (In other words, everything is marketing.)
- And last, dentistry is one of the best investments people can make, and most of them don't know that.

I'll keep circling back to those ideas and referring back to sections from my previous book, but in this book we are going to go much further into the concepts, systems, and behavior that can make you remarkable.

Throughout the book, I will feature profiles on some dentists I have found to be remarkable. What is fascinating, along with their wonderful practices, is how different each one is. Some have moved completely into accepting most dental plans, while another dropped all but one. One operates a huge, sprawling facility, and others only have one associate.

Some have crazy stuff like heated toilet seats in the restroom, while others just create such deep personal relationships with patients that they could work out of a shipping container and still succeed. I think you will find each of them inspiring in their own way, demonstrating that your vision can vary, but patient experience will always rule the day.

In the end, I gauged their remarkableness by what patients said about them in reviews, which I have included in each profile. These are real quotes—and most of the time I chose longer reviews to demonstrate how much people are willing to say about a practice that gave them a unique, unexpected, and positive, experience.

I'm going to give you a lot of practical tools and information that you can incorporate into your overall practice and your daily actions as a dental team member. But the main thrust of this book is going to be a quantum leap in business thinking and how that applies to the future of your dental practice. Ready to become remarkable? Then let's go!

SECTION ONE:
THE NEW WORLD
DISORDER

CHAPTER 1

TECTONIC
SHIFTS

The dental world is changing. And this isn't a subtle change, but a tectonic shift in the practice of dentistry. There are three main forces at work causing this shift: the expansion of corporate dentistry, the rapid evolution of dental technology, and the explosion of digital communication.

These forces are also the reason you need to become remarkable. Let's look at each one in turn.

CORPORATE DENTISTRY

Corporate dentistry has come a long way. Back in the late 1990s, there was a strong movement in this direction, but most attempts were misguided, failing to provide anything but discounts on consumables and some other savings generated by group buying power and centralized billing. It doesn't take a math whiz to figure out that if consumables average a mere

3 percent of the practice gross revenue, then even saving half (which never happened) would not result in any significant profit. They turned dentist owners into employees and—not so amazingly—their production went down. And there was no broadband Internet connection yet, so there was no way to connect all the practices and facilitate processes like reporting, billing, and insurance filing. So many groups failed, some of them spectacularly.

That is not what's happening now. Group practices are succeeding, some of them spectacularly. In part this is due to smarter businesspeople getting involved. But it also is the new climate. Students are graduating with loans averaging more than $250,000. Add on the cost of continually upgrading technology and the time required to be trained to use it. Finally, it has become a major challenge to promote a practice, with advertising and marketing becoming a fast-moving target. So the appeal of joining a group practice as a new dentist has never been higher.

This is compounded by the fact that the difficulty of running a solo practice has never been greater. Many dentists are deciding they'd rather just do dentistry without the headaches of managing a business, so they sell their practices to a chain.

Group practices range in size from two or three facilities to the largest (at the time of this printing) of 700 or more. They represent more than 15 percent of practices and are growing at a much faster pace than dentistry overall. In fact, group practices now hire 50 percent of dental school graduates. But don't get me wrong. I don't have a judgment about them either way.

I've seen some extremely well-run groups where most of the dentists are very happy, and others where neither the patients nor the dentists are satisfied. But the fact is, this time they are not going away. They are a growing competitive force to be reckoned with. So you will need a strategy to deal with them—either as a successful participant or a thriving competitor.

TECHNOLOGICAL ADVANCES

The next major shift is the proliferation of new technologies. Or rather, the maturing of technologies that have existed for some time. CEREC® has been around for more than 30 years, but only in recent years have the margins reached a point where they are as good or better than a lab can do. The imaging in digital radiography is now much better than film, with much greater speed, utility and convenience, and significantly less radiation. Dental lasers now serve a wide range of purposes. And 3-D imaging is revolutionizing the delivery of implants and orthodontics. The list goes on, and the need to learn and adapt becomes more urgent as it becomes more daunting. These technological advances will be a recurring theme throughout this book, as they represent unique challenges, while at the same time presenting marvelous marketing opportunities.

DIGITAL EVERYTHING

Finally, digital communication is affecting everything. Texting is the most rapidly adopted communication modality in the history of mankind. Over the course of 25 years, we've gone from using cell phones that were attached to our cars to essentially abandoning our home phones. The postal service sends virtually no significant mail, while we send 100 billion emails every day. And we use our phones as Internet search devices, cameras, game consoles, TVs, social media connections, GPS devices (and occasionally even still make phone calls with them). And we use them to read and write reviews of every business we interact with.

Is all this change a good thing? Like surfing, that depends where you are in the wave, and how well you surf.

CHAPTER 2

DISRUPTING
DENTISTRY

I'm going to throw a big and perhaps scary idea at you. There is
a rule in business that has existed for almost as long as capital-
ism itself, which is essentially the "faster, better, cheaper rule."
The principle is that your business can only be two of those
three things at once. You can't be the best and cheapest and
still be the fastest. McDonald's is often given as the example,
where it's fast and cheap, and so the quality of the food has to
be sacrificed. This paradigm has held true for centuries.

"Better" is sometimes hard to define, and "faster" generally either applies to the speed of the service or how fast a product is
made or delivered. "Cheaper" is a lot easier to gauge, but people
also value things differently, so it's not always exact. The explicit
point was: You will succeed if you focus on excelling at two of
these things. Implicit was that doing all three was not possible.

All around us, that rule is being disrupted. For example, isn't
Google™ Maps faster, better, and cheaper than the old Thomas

Guide® or AAA maps? I would argue that it is extremely so in each category. Now think about books. A new novel can be delivered to my phone in two minutes—even at 2am—costing half the price of the hardcover version. Plus, it's searchable, looks up definitions with the tap of a finger, remembers where I left off, and can now synchronize with the audiobook version I'm listening to. How is my Kindle® not significantly faster, better, *and* cheaper?

It's not just software, either. When I travel to the airport from my house, I use Uber®, the car service that is sweeping the planet. An Uber driver shows up in less than five minutes with a nice clean car and takes me to LAX for half what a taxi would have cost. Half. And then I get out and don't have to deal with the tip or fumble with my credit card. I just get out. It's all paid through the phone app automatically. How is that not faster, better, and cheaper? In fact, it's better than a taxi in so many ways I can't even list them here.

The examples go on and on. The video camera in my phone. Netflix®. And let's talk about health care. Artificial intelligence (AI) and robotics are going to profoundly affect the delivery of medicine. I recently saw a video where a robot stitched the peel back onto a grape. That's precision. And robots never get tired or show up with a hangover. And AI will have access to all medical information and eventually diagnose better than a physician. Many surgeries will soon cost a fraction of what they do now.

What is required in any business is not just a system, but a belief—a mindset—that this approach is achievable. Once you adopt this mindset, then all it requires is taking a close look at what the consumer wants, and then using technology—both hardware and software—to do something differently, something better, faster, and cheaper.

Let me bring up one more disruptive element that relates directly to my overall point. It is now easier than ever to find the cheapest version of anything. Want the least expensive Lasik surgeon? Just Google "lowest price Lasik" and you'll get 20 pages of results. Transparent prices are becoming the norm, whether businesses like it or not. You can find out the manufacturer's cost of a car or the cheapest place to get your next TV. Case in point, Best Buy® now agrees to match the price you can find online for a product, just to keep their business from turning into a showroom for online dealers.

It is only a matter of time before much of what we charge for in dentistry becomes public and searchable. Despite the fact that costs and insurance reimbursements vary widely from city to city and state to state, dental consumers are going to be able to comparison shop. That's the first reason why you need to become more affordable.

The bigger reason is to broaden the marketplace by making it possible for a greater percent of the population to afford dental care. By the way, cheaper doesn't mean you make less money. You simply have to be more efficient, because your business is about what you produce in any given hour. Imagine if we brought implants to the masses—and used existing technology to deliver them faster, better, and cheaper—so that the average blue collar worker didn't have to look forward to a lifetime of dentures. If you are faster, you can charge less and make the same profit. Maybe more.

And as I will discuss further in the book, better dentistry is relative. But if you can deliver dentistry faster and cheaper, at the same level quality, that will appeal to an enormous segment of the population that is currently avoiding you because of time and money.

Some people will argue with me that you can't really excel at all three—that you can't be the fastest, the best, and the cheapest. But as I've said, I guarantee you an Uber ride is faster, better, and cheaper than any taxi ride you've ever taken. So all three are achievable. Will it be possible in dentistry? Could you deliver high-quality treatment, get the patient out of the office in less time, and make it more affordable by being a highly efficient practice? I believe this is possible right now.

This mindset is the pathway to becoming remarkable. Uber, Kindle, and Netflix are experiencing explosive growth because people *talk about them!* Their products are so unique in all three ways that people can't resist sharing the experience of using them. Their phenomenal success is due more to people sharing how much they love their products than about any promotions they are doing. And when they do promote themselves, the new customers are delighted, and discover even more reasons to like the services—and they tell everyone they know. Sound like a great way to build a dental practice?

I know this can be disturbing and daunting to think about. But it doesn't make it less true. In fact, it makes it all the more important not to ignore this inevitable shift. It's not a matter of whether this will happen in dentistry, it's when. How soon? I can't give you an exact time frame, but wouldn't you like to be ahead of the curve? This book is all about how you can create a better dental experience, do dentistry faster, and provide it more affordably, while earning more than you do now, but with a much more secure future.

So let me do a simple breakdown of how you can execute this strategy, so that you can see how possible it really is.

FASTER

Faster applies in several areas. Clinical dentistry can certainly be faster with CAD/CAM. One visit versus two. Faster for you and faster for the patient. CBCT allows for single-visit implants for a number of cases, but every case goes faster. Lasers reduce the number of perio treatment visits. In essence, change isn't just accelerating, it's accelerating treatment.

BETTER

To me that means more efficient, more convenient, more enjoyable, more trustworthy. And again, higher quality clinically because of your technology and training. You remove less tissue when you don't have to build a temporary. You don't have redos on a bad fit from the lab work. With implants, you're not cutting a flap anymore. And lasers cure perio, rather than just maintain it. But better really means an extraordinary overall experience more than just a clinical one. And that's doable right now.

CHEAPER

Let's relabel cheaper as "more affordable" from now on. If you can reduce the treatment time, you can reduce the cost and still make a profit. You don't have to even reduce it in the same proportion as the time you're saving. Totally unnecessary. If you can utilize your facility better by having more dentists working more hours, your overhead is reduced as a percentage, and you can reduce your fees, because your profit margin has gone up considerably. And efficiently presenting financing makes you more affordable.

SO NOW WHAT?

Simple. Adopt the mindset that you and your team can deliver dentistry faster, better, and more affordably than before, and that your goal in doing this is to become so remarkable that your patients can't resist talking about you.

And then do everything in this book and my last one.

CHAPTER 3

THE PATIENT EXPERIENCE IS PARAMOUNT

THE LESSON OF KODAK

In 1996, Eastman Kodak® was worth over $30 billion and was considered the fifth most valuable brand in the world. In September 2013—just 17 years later—this 125-year-old company filed for bankruptcy, its shares worth nothing. Zero.

How did this happen? In the beginning, George Eastman started with a brilliant idea: Make photography easier and more portable. It worked. Over the years, the business evolved and Kodak began to believe that its business was about making better and better photographic film. And it dominated the film photography industry. However, in the process, it completely ignored the onset of digital photography.

Unfortunately, in the end, film wasn't what people really cared about. We all have boxes of photos that we never look at. What people really like to do is take and share photos as easily, often, and quickly as possible. We don't just take pictures for ourselves, we take them to show other people. George Eastman wanted to bring photography to the masses. Digital photography does that much more easily than film ever could. The company wandered away from Eastman's guiding principle, believing it was in the film business, when it was in the photo sharing business. Ironically, it was Kodak who invented the first digital camera back in 1975 and then abandoned its development. Oops.

In a further twist of irony, three months after Kodak went bankrupt, Instagram®, a simple phone application designed to enhance photos on cell phones, sold to Facebook for $1 billion after only two years of operation and *not a single dollar of revenue!* Why? Because the creators of Instagram clearly understood two things: consumer desire and digital technology.

What is the lesson here for dentistry? It is twofold. Kodak lost sight of what the consumer was really looking for, and it also failed to adapt the disruptive technology that was encroaching on their empire until it was too late. I see many dentists making this same mistake. They believe that their dental skill is what attracts patients, when what patients care about is the experience of being in the practice. And many dentists feel that they can ignore the advances in dental technology and ride out the next 10 or 20 years with the same facility that they started their practice with.

This is what I call "ostrich dentistry," believing that if you ignore the changes occurring all around you that they won't affect you. It didn't work for Kodak, and it's not working in many industries. We live in an era of constant disruption.

So how does this relate to dentistry? Quite closely, in fact. I meet many dentists who still believe that if they just become better clinically then this will automatically get them more patients. Some were even told this by their ivory-tower professors in dental school. The truth is, if you build it, they still won't come. Most people do not know how to evaluate a dentist's clinical skills. But they can evaluate the experience of being in the practice. In about 10 seconds.

People can't assess a dentist's clinical skills, But they can quickly and easily assess the experience of being in the practice.

I learned this one absolute truth in my 30 years of interacting with dental patients. Because they have no way of assessing your clinical skills, they are forced to evaluate you based on the experience of being your patient. A less-than-amazed patient may continue to go to you, because they dread the idea of finding a new dentist (another fact we've learned over the years), but they are unlikely to recommend you if the experience of being your patient is not positive.

WORD OF THUMB

This fact about patient experience is being reinforced—and in fact amplified—by online reviews. When you read reviews on Yelp or Google, you will never find a review that says, "This dentist's margins were way off," or "She didn't check my occlusion before designing my veneers." It's always about the experience of interacting with you and your team, and the environment of the office. They'll say, "The dentist really explained everything so well," or "They're always running late and no one seems to care," or "Everyone who works there is so nice and friendly," or "This dentist just wants to make money."

In fact, the number one question I get from dentists when I'm out lecturing is, "How can I get a bad review down from Yelp?"

The short answer is, "You can't." Only the person who posted it can take it down.

The long answer is, "You need an overall strategy for dealing with online reviews." You can win the online review battle— and it is a battle, make no mistake—with a systematic approach to generating reviews, responding to them, and leveraging them to your advantage.

How did all this happen so quickly? Again, there's a short answer: smart phones. Everyone is carrying a device with Internet access and applications that allow them to easily find and write reviews for anything they want to do or buy. Word of mouth has turned into word of thumb. But even more important is that it has become something permanent.

Now opinions are searchable, "likable," and "sharable." Welcome to the digital world. The solution, of course, is to be remarkable.

Here are the hallmarks of a remarkable practice, and what drives the patient experience, in order:

- An amazing, friendly, helpful team that enjoys what they do
- Excellent communication skills
- Comfort-conscious and convenience-focused technology
- A practice environment that is soothing, relaxing, and pleasing to every sense
- Convenient hours and access
- Advanced clinical skills and a wide range of services

In short, a remarkable practice is completely patient-centric.

It starts with the website, social media, and the phone skills of your front desk people. And is carried through by everything else that patients see, hear, taste, touch, and smell in your practice. From the design of your reception to your scrubs to the words you use.

Loyalty is harder than ever to gain with patients. They expect convenience, a nice atmosphere, and ease of payment. Because of this, a number of dental practices are about to have their own "Kodak moment," when their value gradually diminishes to essentially nothing. Their patients will have left and will have not told them why.

So I'm telling you why. If you think you don't need a nice reception area, a clean, technologically advanced practice, a friendly staff, an active Facebook presence, and a dynamic website, you're fooling yourself. The decline of your practice will be gradual, until it's rapid. Think I'm way off base? Ask the guy who had a little coffee shop and thought Starbucks wasn't going to affect him. Ask the computer store owner who didn't think Dell computers would change the industry. Ask the film editor who thought digital editing would never catch on.

The deepest core of the patient experience is built on three interlocking practice assets: your team, your technology, and your trustworthiness. When these are solid, everything else gets easy. And when one element is deficient, all your ability to provide a remarkable experience will be severely impaired.

Let me put it another way. Dentistry is not scarce. But a great dental experience is. So by all means, keep taking your clinical courses and getting better at providing high-quality, comfort-conscious dentistry. You're a medical professional. But don't think for a minute that in the next decade that's going to be enough.

CHAPTER 4

IS YOUR
PRACTICE A
TEAR-DOWN?

Most people reduce Darwinism to "survival of the fittest," but his theory actually states that the species that survives is the one that is most adaptable.

And let's face it—humans are not the fittest species. We couldn't outrun a house cat, we swim slower than a goldfish, and we need clothing to keep from freezing to death. Half of us need glasses to even be able to *see* clearly. We are the only mammal that needs to straighten our teeth. And yet we dominate the planet for one reason: We are highly adaptive.

But like most species, we only adapt when we need to. We resist change, we ignore impending doom, and sometimes we legislate against change. But change comes anyway. (Witness the battle going on over corporate dentistry in various states.)

Well, in dentistry today the need to evolve has reached a much higher level of urgency.

Because my company deals with dental consumers all over the country, dentists often ask me what I think the future of dentistry will be. One of the first things I tell them is that I believe that within a generation the solo dental practice will not be a sustainable business model. More on that a little later. But the second thing I tell them is that if they don't improve and expand their services and technology—and refresh their patient base and their facility—they won't have a practice to sell in 10 years.

In dentistry today the need to evolve has reached a high level of urgency.

Despite this, I meet dentists every week who are hoping to coast to the end of their practice run without upgrading their facility, spending any money to attract new patients, or offering any sort of convenient hours, yet are still hoping to get a nice payday when they sell their practice.

Let me ask you, if you were selling your home, would you just put it on the market without painting it, doing some landscaping, throwing out that pile of magazines, and getting rid of that beat-up couch in the living room? Would you still expect to get full value for your house?

Yet this is exactly what dentists are doing all across the country. And what happens is a new dentist will no longer buy that existing practice. He'll just open across the street with a new facility, convenient hours, and single-visit dentistry, and vacuum half the patients out of that other practice in a year or two.

Just because you don't see big changes coming doesn't mean they're not looming on the horizon. I've worked in the dental field half my life, and for the first time I'm witnessing dentists losing their entire practice—just handing the keys over to the bank. Or they sell their practice for 50 percent of one-year's collections. Others declined 30 percent in a single year (2008) and then 5-10 percent every year thereafter.

WHERE ARE YOU IN YOUR CAREER ARC?

So the question becomes, where are you in your career arc and does that match your facility? To continue the housing metaphor, are you new construction, a fixer-upper, or a tear-down? Be honest with yourself.

Scenario one: Let's say you are in the final 10 years of practicing and you haven't bought any new equipment in 20 years. Your entire facility looks like it did when you took it over. And most of your patients are your age or above. Smells like a tear-down to me. Might be time to move to a new location. But if not, it's time to gut the place and market to get a younger patient base. Bring in an associate. And tech up. Just like with a house, the money will come back in the sale if you do it right.

Scenario two: You're 15-20 years from hanging up your hand piece. Your facility still looks good, and you remodeled the reception area five years ago. You just added digital radiography. You've got decent word of mouth, but there aren't a lot of young faces in the schedule. You're a fixer-upper. Add CEREC and maybe in a year or two CBCT. Advertise to get younger patients in. Take a hard look at your chairs, cabinetry, and flooring, and start a process of upgrades and improvements. Maybe take a look at your team and add some new blood to energize the place. Bring in an associate. And then stay ahead of the wave.

Scenario three: Your practice is a comfortable, new environment with a broad age range of patients. The operatories are bristling with new technology and the team is energized and patients are referring consistently. You're new construction. All you need is an associate.

You get the formula, right? Figure out where you are in the arc of your career and then take a close look at your practice. You will always want to look like new construction. Use this as a lens through which you can prioritize the actions that this book will suggest to you. Then, after a rewarding dental career, you can still reap the full value of your dental practice when you decide to sell.

Dentistry can be a fantastic profession for many years—perhaps many generations to come—but it's evolve or die, just like everything else on the planet.

CHAPTER 5

YOU ARE NOT AN ENTREPRENEUR

This is a good thing. The accurate definition of an entrepreneur is someone who has a vision to do something innovative in a specific industry—either something that hasn't been done yet or something done a completely different way.

A dentist, on the other hand, is a small business owner. You are essentially self-employed. This means that you don't have to invent a new approach to your industry. The most successful ways of running a dental business already exist—you simply have to put those into practice. They are known, they are learnable, and the results have been demonstrated.

The pinnacle of this is to become a remarkable dental practice. Throughout this book I'm going to give you examples of remarkable practices. You will see that, although bold choices were made and risks were taken, they did not reinvent dentistry. You don't have to either, but you may have to reinvent yourself. This goes for the dentist and the team members as well. And when you do, it might be scary, but it will prove to be rewarding and satisfying, a challenge worthy of the effort.

Also, I think dentists deserve to be wealthy. This is America, after all, and if you work hard and provide a valuable service, then you should be well paid. Don't get me wrong, it's not that I think that everyone who is wealthy deserves to be. I think there are a whole lot of people who make money on the shoulders of other people's hard work, who contribute nothing to the economy, but just take from it. But you keep people healthy. Why is that not valuable? Why is that not deserving of a wealthy lifestyle? With all the education and training and investment required, it's only right that you make a comfortable living.

Surgeons make great money, and very few people complain about it. Dentists are surgeons and should accordingly be rewarded with wealth, as well. But let me get a little philosophical here. Wealth isn't just about money. It's about making enough money to live the way you would like while doing something that fulfills you. Because if your work isn't fulfilling, there isn't enough money in the world for you to be truly happy. I'm hoping to show you ways to make your practice intensely fulfilling and financially rewarding. And you may even enjoy reinventing yourself and start to make a habit of it.

So let's get into the economic realities of a dental practice in the 21st Century. The game is changing…

CHAPTER 6

THE END OF
TWO ERAS

THE END OF THE SOLO PRACTITIONER

There are two factors that have convinced me that the solo practitioner business model will be an indefensible model within the next decade or two. The first, probably quite obviously, is the expansion of group practices and corporate dentistry. The challenge for any solo practitioner is a lack of business skill coupled with a lack of time to learn and apply those skills, especially when, to earn money, the dentist has to be working with her hands, treating patients. Corporate dentistry doesn't have that problem. They have people with the requisite business skills handling the business aspects of their practices.

They can be more efficient in a number of ways, freeing up the dentists to do more actual dentistry. They can advertise more effectively, schedule more efficiently, and deal with hiring, firing, billing, compliance, and a host of other business activities.

And they can even train dentists and team members as groups, which will also increase production.

The other factor is double-edged. A solo practitioner can only do dentistry so many hours a week. But dental facilities are essentially surgical suites, and the advances in technology have reached a point where approximately 5 percent of your revenue should be allocated to staying current with new technology. This means that overhead is greater than before, yet the dentist is using the surgical suite only a fraction of the time. This requires the solo dentist to produce more just to break even.

The other difference is that the soloist has a much greater challenge being convenient and being accessible whenever his patients need him. The dentist has to be willing to work evenings, early mornings, and Saturdays in order to compete. And every vacation means the office is not producing, plus the dentist is unavailable for emergencies or new patients. This is not a problem corporate dentistry experiences.

Does my prediction change when you add associates? Definitely, but only when you add convenience to the mix. You still need to maximize your facility. To me the ideal strategy— if you don't want to become part of a larger group—is to have at least two associates or GP partners, and a couple of specialists in the office, as well as some itinerant specialists who come in three or four times a month.

Within a generation, I believe solo practices will be less than 20 percent of dentistry.

My projection is that solo practices will be less than 20 percent of dentistry within a generation. If I'm wrong, it will only be by the percentage.

THE END OF THE FEE-FOR-SERVICE-ONLY PRACTICE

Back in 2000, it was the goal of many dental practices to become full fee-for-service and stop accepting all insurance plans. And for a while, it worked, because there was more disposable income and people could also charge their restorative and cosmetic dentistry to their home equity line of credit. But then in 2007 the mortgage and banking crisis hit. That money disappeared within a matter of months.

Along with that, dental insurance companies are also initiating a major disruption. Across the country, state by state, they are cutting reimbursements and dictating care, supposedly to make premiums more affordable, although the evidence seems to indicate that executive bonuses went up and premiums stayed the same. This is coupled with a major shift in dental consumer behavior.

Starting in 2008, in our call center at 1-800-DENTIST®, we noticed a dramatic shift in patients' willingness to go out of network. Whereas before, more than 80 percent would be willing to go out of network for the right dentist, now it's less than 20 percent. And this is true at every income level. No matter what segment of the population, they want as much treatment paid for by someone else as possible.

We've noticed some other changes as well. For lack of a better description, it seems that patients are flakier than ever. They ignore or forget appointments, change them at the last minute, and will often only want to do treatment that is covered by their insurance, and more people than ever are seeing a dentist only on an emergency basis.

In 2013, 59.3 percent of the U.S. population supported their family on less than $50,000 in household—yes, household—income. And 15 percent of the population lives below the poverty line.[1] So it's really no mystery why 50 percent of the population doesn't see a dentist regularly. $1,800 for a root canal and crown? Forget it. It's extraction time.

So you have to take a hard look at your demographics and patient base, decide how you want to grow, and how hard you want to work (because you will obviously make less money for your services on PPO patients), and you need to have good skills to communicate the value of the dentistry beyond basic covered care. But know that as of 2013, according to the National Association of Dental Plans, 86 percent of private practitioners accept at least one PPO. The tide has already turned.

There are several successful economic approaches to dental practices. You can even be successful accepting State Aid. Or be HMO-based. But it involves different strategies and standards of care. And you have to accept the need to match that care with what your demographic can afford.

But I don't believe that this trend of patients insisting on staying in network is going to ever reverse itself. If anything, with so much focus on universal health care in the past years, it's going to become even more entrenched in consumer behavior.

WHY AM I STILL OPTIMISTIC?

So full-fee-for-service is dead. The solo practice is becoming an insupportable business model. Discretionary income is down at every level of American society except the top 10 percent. Health care overall is in disarray, with dentistry still on the outside looking in. And dental school is disproportionately expensive. So why am I so optimistic?

Because human lifespan is increasing steadily. And people will want their teeth. And that first group of people living longer—baby boomers—is experiencing the largest transfer of wealth in the history of mankind. They will not only pay for their dentistry, but their kids' dentistry. (Hey, they let them drink Coke growing up—time to pay the piper!)

I often say that dentistry is the most resilient business model in the country. This is true because of the basic necessity of tooth care. While many people cannot afford comprehensive care, they eventually will need some kind of treatment. The opportunity is there. And technology is going to make it possible for most dentists to deliver dentistry faster, better, and more affordably than ever, to a larger group of patients.

But dentistry is also highly resilient because of the uniqueness of the dental practice economic model. So let's examine that.

CHAPTER 7

ESCAPING GRAVITY

THE BEAUTY OF DENTAL PRACTICE ECONOMICS

On a manned space flight to Mars (which is 34 million miles away), 50 percent of the fuel would be used to go the first 400 miles. The reason for that, of course, is how much energy it takes just to escape Earth's gravity. In many ways this parallels starting and operating a dental practice.

The gravity is your list of fixed expenses: rent, equipment leases, loan payments, utilities, salaries, etc. Until you "escape gravity," that is, produce enough to pay your fixed expenses, your practice profit for the month is $0. After that, you are able to keep an exceptional amount of the collections for that month, because for the most part your variable expenses—lab costs and supplies—is less than 20 percent of your fees.

This is very different from many other businesses. In most retail stores, for example, the fixed expenses are less than 20 percent, and the variable costs, like the stuff they put on the shelves, is close to 70 percent. If they sell a lot more in a given month, they still only keep 10-20 percent of what goes in the till.

The challenge for many dentists is that their practice is barely escaping gravity. The team works hard at "cracking the nut" every month, and the accountant tells the dentist that her overhead (calculated by all costs except what the dentist pays him or herself) is 70 percent. So the dentist thinks that for every dollar she produces going forward, she is only going to keep 30 cents.

That could not be further from the truth.

Once you escape gravity, you keep 80 percent of the *increase* in production. This economic fact is one of the most beautiful things about the dental practice model. For example, say a practice is producing $40,000 per month, (which in the average urban area would still be trapped in fixed-expense gravity) and the profit margin is 30 percent. That leaves $12,000 for the dentist. Now imagine production is increased by $8,000 in the following month. Then the economics change significantly.

How? Simple. Because on that additional $8,000, the only expenses are variable ones: lab costs, consumables, and perhaps a few extra hours of employee time. Even a high estimate of those costs would come out to only 20 percent of that $8,000.

Which means $6,400 is additional profit. The dentist's monthly income went from $12,000 to $18,400. Total production only increased by 20 percent, but the profit margin has now gone from 30 percent to 38 percent. And the dentist's income has increased by more than 50 percent!

This is why the more successful practices can do more marketing, bonus their teams more, add new technology, and upgrade their facility, further improving the efficiency, appeal, and success of the practice. It is not unusual for a dental practice producing over $800,000 to operate at less than 60 percent overhead.

I'm writing about this because I often encounter dentists who are thinking about advertising to get new patients (or using 1-800-DENTIST), and they make a calculation on the return on investment based on a flat-line perception of their overhead percentage. But the production on those new patients is at your "escaped gravity" percentage, which means you can afford to invest in your growth at a much higher level. You may pay $200 or $300 for a new patient, but if the lifetime value of a patient is $5,000, and your true profit is 80 percent, you've invested $300 to make $4,000 in additional profit.

Do you think group practices understand this formula? You can bet they do. And if you want to compete effectively with them, you'd better understand it too. And if you want to join them, the economics are there to justify the endeavor.

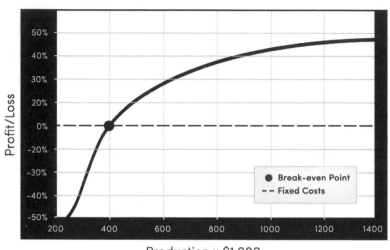

Escaping Gravity

Production x $1,000

The graph here shows how, unlike many businesses where the profit margin levels off much more quickly, in dentistry it can reach 40% before that happens. Pretty remarkable, I'd say.

And isn't this unique economic opportunity good motivation for getting better at what you do—and increasing your production? Does it not make sense to incentivize your team to get the practice to escape gravity every month, and more every year? By the way, this is also where your economic freedom will come from. It's a lot easier to save 10 percent of your income when your profit margin is 40 percent than when it's 25 percent.

There are thousands of practices that do this every month, and they don't have some magic bullet marketing trick. Okay, they do, but it's not some secret Google AdWords formula or miraculous direct mail offer. It's this: *consistently creating a great patient experience.* In short, being remarkable. And that may not be easy, but it's doable. And when the rewards are this stratospheric (you know I had to complete the metaphor somehow!), then it's worth the focus.

CHAPTER 8

YOU MAKE YOUR
OWN ECONOMY

I've been lucky enough in my life to encounter very successful business people—many who've far exceeded my achievements—and they all operated from this one principle: Focus on what is in your control. They understood that when it comes to your business, you make your own economy.

What that means is be aware of what is going on in your world and what affects your business, but don't waste any energy on those things that are out of your control. Modify and adapt to conditions, but don't let outside factors that you can't change drain your positive energy and determination.

Here's how I apply that myself: I can't control the elections in my state or the country. I can't solve the European debt problems. I can't control unemployment. Or gas prices. Or when the next recession will be. So I focus on what our business needs to do, how it needs to evolve, and who we need working with us to achieve our goals and discover new ones.

There are so many businesses that started in economic downturns. Apple®, Microsoft®, FEDEX®, and CNN®, to name a few. And you can thrive in a downturn as well. Zappos®, the online clothing store, grew in 10 years to $1 billion in revenue by 2007. Then the recession hit. Tony Hsieh, the CEO, then grew their business to $2 billion in three more years. Why? Because his attention was on *his* economy. He knew where to focus 100 percent of his energy and to ignore the doom and gloom predictions around him.

If the fluctuations of the Dow Jones Average controls your attitude about the economy, ignore it. Unless you are a day trader, you need to forget about it. You can't control it. No one really has any idea why a stock goes up or down. "Past results are not predictors of future performance." How many times have you heard that? I call this the Tao of Ignoring the Dow, which translates to the peacefulness that comes from not being distracted by the negative noise of the world.

You may not be able to solve the world's problems, but you can make a real difference when you contribute a positive business to the world.

You only have so much positive, productive energy. If something that you can't do anything about drains that energy, then you need to stop paying attention to it. If watching CNN® bums you out, stop watching it. It's pointless negative input. You are never going to solve the Middle East crisis or the banking crisis. You are not going to control the outcome of a political election. Most of us can't even convince our own spouse not to cancel out our vote.

So why make that your input?

Business requires determination and persistence, but our will-power is finite and is diminished by negativity. You cannot remain optimistic and determined to succeed in the face of constant negative input. You control this incredible business—this beautiful ecosystem that is your dental practice—that makes great money while helping people in a profound way, a way few people get to do.

Making your own economy comes down to some very simple operative principles.

Being disciplined. This doesn't mean being rigid, but rather being consistent about adhering to your values, no matter what the situation.

Learning Continuously. As important as ignoring the noise is gathering the positive input and valuable information relevant to your business wherever you can. From your peers, from great speakers, and writers, and from your coworkers.

Being Cautiously Optimistic. Hope and aim for the best outcome, but be prepared for some things not to work out, and don't expect things to always go your way. Don't leave yourself without cash reserves, and don't adhere to practice behaviors that have outlived their value as the marketplace evolves.

Practice the Tao of Ignoring the Dow, and focus your energy on those things that you can affect. You may not be able to solve all the world's problems, but you make a real difference when you contribute a positive business to the world.

THE EVOLVING
DENTAL PATIENT

REMARKABLE DENTIST #1

Paul M. Neilson, DDS
Life Smiles Dental Care
Phoenix, AZ
lifesmilesdentalcare.com
facebook.com/lifesmilesdentalcare

Year opened: 2007, fully remodeled in 2011

REMARKABLE NUMBERS:

Average annual growth since 2007: 25 percent
New patients per month: 65
Dropped 33 dental plans, only keeping 1
Google reviews: 108, adding 2 more each week
Associates: 2

Dr. Neilson's 25 percent average growth rate over 7 years is even more remarkable when you consider that one of the years—2008—the practice only grew 3 percent.

REMARKABLE BEHAVIOR:

Every day in the morning huddle they read a patient review that features one of the team members.

Every new patient gets a tour of the practice.

The team uses its software to store images of patients so that they can be easily recognized and greeted by name— and the patient records are filled with personal information so that team members are able to make a personal connection with every single patient in every visit.

Any patient who has had a treatment requiring anesthesia will be called by one of the dentists in the evening, without fail.

None of these behaviors is extraordinary by themselves. What is remarkable is that at Life Smiles, they do *all* of them, consistently. And it shows in their online reviews.

REMARKABLE QUOTE:

The dentists all use digital photography to show the patient on a monitor exactly what is going on in their mouth. Dr. Neilson says, "This takes them from thinking about their teeth to thinking about their smile."

WHAT PEOPLE SAY:

"Any long-standing aversion to going to a dentist can now be thrown out the window. Life Smiles Dental Care is on a whole other level, in the best way possible."

"Upon walking in, you are greeted by a friendly staff member and then taken on a tour around the office. The office is immaculately clean and modern, with all the latest technology. Once you are seated and go through X-rays, you are given a remote to watch any TV program you would like (old school dentists all around the world are currently cringing; we are smiling). The TV is then used to show you exactly what is going on in your mouth and how exactly they are going to fix it."

"I had had some similar work done in the past with another dentist and there were long-term sensitivity issues that changed my eating habits for some time. This time with Dr. Neilson—ZERO issues—excellent work. I've seen him in the past as well, but I've strayed elsewhere for price and proximity and it just isn't worth it."

"Always a warm greeting as I come through the door— greeted by name! Heidi invariably comes by to greet me and to give us an opportunity to talk about our respective travel plans... She's a delight. This most recent visit, Dr. Paul came to greet me in the waiting room; professional and cordial, sincerely interested and also interesting."

CHAPTER 9

WHAT MATTERS
TO PATIENTS

The most important thing in any business is understanding what your consumer wants. It sounds simple and obvious, but do you really understand what it is that patients want? What their priorities are? To have a remarkable practice, you need to be doing those things that matter most to your patients. AT 1-800-DENTIST, we recently commissioned an independent survey of real dental patients' opinions about dentists and oral health.[2] Combined with our years of experience with dental consumers, some very clear trends emerged. Here are the priorities for patients and what you should most certainly be doing to accommodate those wishes and concerns.

WHAT PATIENTS LIKE

Clear, Honest Conversation about Cost. 90 percent of the patients surveyed expressed the belief that "dental work is expensive." No surprise there. But more than 90 percent also said they are more likely to continue seeing a dentist who engages in an open, honest, and upfront conversation about costs. And one of their biggest frustrations is the practice's unwillingness to discuss fees up front. This is a big challenge, when most consultants will tell you never to discuss fees over the phone. Is this still a viable approach, when cost is such a deciding factor for a new patient? It certainly is one more reason to strive to provide more affordable treatment. And whatever you do, don't start treatment before the patient is fully aware of the costs involved and how much their dental plan should cover.

Dovetailing with this priority is the belief that dentists try to sell patients unnecessary treatment. In the survey, 31 percent of respondents believed this to be true. So the best solution is to be very clear in your discussion with patients about what is optional versus what is necessary.

They Want What They Want. I have some family and friends who live in Thailand, so when I would visit there I would bring a suitcase full of American items, such as Sonicare® toothbrushes, Tide to Go®, Doritos®, and various other bizarre items. My sister-in-law in particular loved Junior Mints®, so I brought several boxes over, as they are not available in Bangkok. One year, I decided to give her a real treat and brought her some expensive Ghirardelli® Chocolates with peppermint, just so she could experience the next level of quality and flavor. I gave them to her and she was polite and grateful. But the following year, she told me, "Just bring Junior Mints this time."

How often do we do that—automatically assume a patient wants high-end dentistry when all they really want is basic care? It's important to keep in mind that many patients don't need premium-level dentistry. They don't all need a perfect smile. Some of them have a smile that we can barely look at, but they don't really care. As long as they can chew their food, they're fine.

And we have to be okay with that. Obviously you want to keep your patients informed on treatment that is going to preserve and protect their dentition, but not everyone wants veneers or cares how white their teeth are. They aren't going to die if their teeth aren't perfect. Often we try to impose our own sensibilities on other people or believe that everyone wants the best of everything.

A whole lot of people are content with average, are comfortable with it, and maybe even prefer it. They're still going to need restorative dentistry as they age, but they need to know that you're okay doing the minimum, not the maximum.

Apply the Junior Mints Principle and your patients will be happier with you because you gave them what they wanted, not what you wanted to give them.

I'll give you another example. My cousin Michael sells used cars. He is a great salesman and knows how to get someone excited about buying a car. But he also knows that some people just need reliable transportation for as little money as possible. So he determines this fairly quickly and doesn't try to sell them more than they need or can really afford. Because of this he has hundreds of repeat customers who trust him. And when they have more money, then he can sell them a car with more features. Do I even have to draw the analogy here?

When you're discussing the patient's priorities, this is where you can learn how important their smile is to them. Certainly you want to spend the time necessary to elevate the value of a healthy mouth in their mind. But many people don't care how white or straight their teeth are. They just want to be able to chew, and they don't want their teeth to hurt or fall out. That's it. My sister-in-law was remarkably unimpressed with high-end sweets. Apply the Junior Mints Principle when talking to your patients, and they'll be happier with you, because you gave them what they wanted, not what you wanted to give them.

Don't forget also that value is a perception. You don't have to be the cheapest dentist if the experience of seeing you enhances their perception of value. But they will trust you much more if you are open about the expense involved, and give them a clear sense of what is optional and desirable rather than essential treatment. I'll repeat this once again: You can only be remarkable if they trust you.

Convenience. In a world with ATMs everywhere, overnight shipping from Amazon®, and 24-hour supermarkets, this should not come as a surprise. Convenience encompasses many aspects of your practice. I will go into more detail on this in Chapter 33, but here are some important facts to remember. In the survey, nearly half the patients wanted weekend hours. What's more, 74 percent of new patients want to be able to see a dentist right away. And yet studies show that less than 40 percent of practices actually appoint new patients within 48 hours.[3] Do you see the massive disconnect here? And we also know from internal research that the further out you schedule new patients, the greater the odds of them becoming a no-show. And you know what that does to your production.

So have convenient hours. I'm going to mention this often, because it's also part of your defensive strategy against any type of competition, whether it's a group or just a small practice that is willing to do what it takes to attract new patients. I know two young dentists who opened a practice from scratch in San Francisco, and they opened from 7am to 7pm, Tuesday through Saturday. They split the shifts, so they each only worked a 30-hour week. But within a year, the schedule was entirely full. Even more significant is that they did no other promotion of their practice. All it took was convenient hours and their practice was booming. Convenience is good marketing.

With this in mind, CEREC is a great convenience tool as well. If you don't think that one visit versus two is more appealing, then I don't know what to tell you. Remember, the second visit isn't just another set of shots and drilling, it's another slot of time out of work along with the drive back and forth to your office. There is nothing convenient about it. And just imagine if the crown doesn't fit (which it doesn't 6 percent of the time, on average). Now it's doubly inconvenient.

Real Reviews. The reason the focus of this book is becoming a remarkable practice is because of this simple fact: More than 70 percent of consumers say that ratings and reviews influence their choice of a dentist. And many say that reviews are just as important as the dentist's credentials.

People can find reviews of you on Yelp, Google, Facebook, HealthGrades®, Angie's List®, and several other places. You need a systematic and continuous strategy for generating, tracking, and responding to reviews. This cannot be neglected or dealt with casually or haphazardly anymore. And your website should have reviews from your patients that have been generated from your own surveys, using automated communication software like Revenue Well Systems®, PatientActivator®, or another application. This is important for both SEO and for patients. Sixty-three percent of consumers say they are more likely to patronize a business if it has reviews on its website.

And great ratings will make it possible for you to charge more for your services. People looking for an excellent dentist care less about the cost than choosing the best dentist for themselves.

Dental Coverage and Financing. Patients overwhelmingly report that they want a dentist to accept their dental insurance and offer financing options. What this means is that you have to have a candid and clear discussion with them up front about the difference between health insurance and dental coverage. Otherwise the trust factor drops. And 80 percent of patients surveyed say insurance is an important factor in choosing a dentist. There is no avoiding it anymore. Also, stop measuring your practice production by the difference between insurance fees and your full fees. You are always going to have to work with what you can actually collect from a patient, not what you could have in a fantasy world of no dental insurance. If you are faster and better at delivering dentistry, then you can simply look at the difference in fees as a marketing cost, part of doing business. And if you are skilled at presenting comprehensive care, there is plenty of dentistry to be done beyond what is covered in most plans.

Your team also has to be comfortable with presenting financing options. In Chapter 31, I go into more detail on this, but you need multiple ways of accommodating your patients' financial situations. Financing is one of the most under-utilized tools in a practice, and 63 percent of dental consumers say financing is an important part of choosing a dentist and accepting treatment.

WHAT PATIENTS DON'T LIKE

Radiation. They may not mention it, but what they do notice is that you cover them with a lead blanket and leave the room before you take an X-ray. They seldom understand that radiation is all around them, and its effects are cumulative. And they don't know what to compare it to. Few realize that the radiation from a digital X-ray is the equivalent of taking a cross-country plane flight. And you don't see flight attendants wearing lead jumpers.

After my last dental cleaning, the hygienist told me, "Next time you come in we'll need to update your X-rays. But we now use digital radiography, which has 80 percent less radiation than the old way." What a brilliant marketing thing to say! Even if I don't know how much radiation I'm getting, 80 percent less sounds better.

Impression materials. Most dentists understand that patients don't like shots or drilling. But they don't like impressions either. A giant ball of goo in their mouth triggers a gag reflex in plenty of people. And the minute it takes to set feels like five. And how often do you do it over? Half the time? Digital impressions are a big positive from the patient standpoint, not just from an accuracy and expediency standpoint.

Mercury. Patients have been told for decades that the mercury is leaking out of their amalgams and causing heavy metal toxicity. Which is why composites have become the norm, even though they don't last as long as amalgams. There are two parts to the solution. The first is to make sure you always use a rubber dam when removing amalgams, and *explain why you're doing it.* They aren't likely to ask about it, but it's reassuring to hear that you are taking that precaution (and they'll wonder why all their previous unremarkable dentists didn't do it!). The second part is solved when you have CAD/CAM in your office and can use porcelain instead of composite for almost any restoration. And, of course, explaining that it will last much longer and match their natural teeth better.

Lack of Cleanliness. Patients are very sensitive to exposure to infectious material when they are in any sort of health care. And they're not wrong. The number one cause of death in a hospital is iatrogenesis, meaning caused by the hospital visit itself.[4] Most often by infection. So make sure every aspect of your practice is pristine clean, from the restroom to the kitchen, and take the time to show patients the sterilization room. They will take great comfort in it.

Poor Time Management. Constantly running behind does not endear your patients to you and is good fodder for bad reviews. If you always seem to be off schedule, get to the bottom of it. It's creating more negative reverberations than you think.

Patients often don't mention these things as factors in their appreciation of you, but part of being remarkable is knowing that these are important, incorporating them into your practice, and clearly communicating the benefits to your patients.

CHAPTER 10

VALUE IS A
PERCEPTION

I'm a huge fan of the business author Simon Sinek. His book *Start with Why* reveals the true key to long-term success for any business. And it's simply this: Great brands—which is what your practice will need to become, by the way—are very clear on why they do what they do. When I get to Chapter 19, I will dive deeper into how you decide this for yourself and bring it to your business.

He also taught me something very important about how consumers behave. It is perhaps the most concise insight I've ever heard in marketing: Value, in the consumer's thought process, is not a *calculation* that they are making about the benefits they receive, but a *perception* of those benefits based on often very subjective factors. I will circle back to this point often. Value is a perception, not a calculation.

Let me give you some examples of this. You will eventually realize that this observation applies to almost every spending event in our lives.

Consider the accessory of chrome wheels on an automobile. If you understand from a technical standpoint what chrome wheels do, you know that they make the car ride rougher, they wear the tires out faster, and they reduce the gas mileage efficiency. So for an extra few thousand dollars, the buyer is making his car *worse* in three ways. So if this were a calculation, it should actually trigger a reduction in value of the car. But the buyer has to have them. Because his perception of the wheels' value is that they enhance his image in other people's minds, and the car is more pleasing to him as he walks up to it (because, of course, the whole time he's using the vehicle he can't see the wheels).

Someone recently paid $2,045,000 at an art auction for a sheet of stationery on which Bob Dylan had written the lyrics to *Like a Rolling Stone.* How could that possibly be a precise calculation someone made? Especially the extra $45,000! Someone's *perception* of the value of that piece of paper was greater than what most people will earn in three decades.

The examples are everywhere. It's estimated that 50 percent of young women in Japan have a Chanel® handbag. Why? Because they believe it makes them stand out. Huh? We buy Nike® products because our favorite athletes display the Nike swoosh on their clothing. And we all know these athletes are *paid* to do this. Some of us even know how much Tiger Woods made last year in endorsement income. And yet we fall for it anyway. It increases our perception of Nike's value, which has nothing to do with how their product is made or performs.

Another example. Whole Foods charges significantly more than Trader Joe's for most of their products. I have been able to discern no difference in the quality of the food, particularly the organic food. But Whole Foods is not suffering. Whole Foods is a lifestyle. People don't just shop there. They dine there. They drink wine there. They drink craft beers there. Trader Joe's, meanwhile, is true to its own brand, in that it offers great value along with great quality.

The parallel here is you can be a Whole Foods type of dental practice or you can be a Trader Joe's type of practice. Both models can be equally thriving and satisfying.

What you *can't* be is nothing. You can't mean nothing to your patients. You create a brand by giving a distinct experience that your patients sincerely believe they cannot get anywhere else. You will not thrive simply by being a tooth repair shop, like they can find on every corner.

You create a brand by giving a distinct experience that your patients sincerely believe they cannot get anywhere else.

My point is, stop thinking that patients should appreciate the value of your dentistry simply because you are well trained and use the best materials. They cannot precisely calculate the value of your skill, or the value of their smile and the increase in health they will enjoy.

What is considered expensive is also a perception that varies widely from person to person. To me, a $17,000 Apple Watch is too expensive. To someone trying to impress people by what they can afford, or how successful they are, it's worth every penny. In the same vein, a perfect smile is worth much more to a successful actress than it is to a construction worker.

Price only dominates our appreciation of a product or service when all we want is the cheapest, regardless of quality. Otherwise, a host of intangible and often unconscious factors come into play. Understanding this is essential in any business. Pretending it's not true—that human beings are completely rational in their decision making and in their responses to situations—is, well, completely irrational.

Think about it.

- Whether you were treated well is a perception.
- Whether you were greeted nicely is a perception.
- Feeling respected is a perception. So is feeling disrespected.
- Feeling talked down to is a perception.
- Feeling understood is a perception.
- Trustworthiness is a perception.
- Feeling appreciated is a perception.

Notice that none of these are calculations people make based on a column of numbers or a list of provable facts.

Listened to me +$57.75
Friendliness +$27.00
Didn't say goodbye -$72.00
Good lighting +$14.00
Made me laugh +$12.00
Friend liked it +$35.00
Rude clerk -$44.50

Most important, they are all integral parts of the patient experience. And the patient experience—much more than the clinical result—is what compels a person to write a positive review, recommend the practice to a friend or family member, or borrow money to get comprehensive treatment. Essentially, customer satisfaction is a key part of the perception of value.

Which is why the little things matter.

Which is why listening is so important.

Which is why price is not the primary factor in patient retention, unless it's the only thing they hear.

Which is why genuinely caring about your patients, more than about making money, matters.

Which is why, quite simply, *everything* matters.

It is these actions that increase customer satisfaction, which increases the perception of value. And this leads me to my next major point, one I hope you can burn into your minds and it drives you to do what it takes to create a remarkable practice. It's this: Dentistry is *subjective* health care.

In *Everything is Marketing,* I made the point that dentistry is *retail* health care, because many of the services you offer are elective. That is, anything a practice does beyond extraction is the next level up of care, and that makes you unique in the medical world, where most times there are one or two treatment solutions. And you can avoid taking care of your teeth your whole life, but if you have a broken leg or breast cancer, you pretty much have to do something about it. Dentistry is on-demand health care, so to speak, more similar to dermatologists and plastic surgeons than general physicians. Because of the lack of medical necessity (in the patient's mind), people often have to be persuaded to do more than the basic treatment.

Now, I'm taking that thinking to the next level. First, appearance is a very subjective issue for people. Some care to an intense level about their teeth—how straight, how white, how much gum recession—and others can be comfortably missing number 9 and don't even wonder what people are staring at. Those are the extremes, but we know that patients are all over the map when it comes to their dental care, most leaning toward neglect and procrastination.

And what's worse is that since people mostly have to pay for their own dentistry, they often make very serious oral health care decisions based almost entirely on cost. This is in contrast to the rest of their bodies, where someone is going to fix whatever's wrong at whatever cost, as long as they pay the co-payment. So they rationalize their irrational, short-term thinking.

And, lastly, enamel is tough. It takes a lot of abuse, and the damage is so gradual that most often it goes unnoticed for decades.

So the burden is on the dentist and the team to amplify the value of good dentistry in the patient's mind. And you also have to help them take a long-term view of their body. Every six months we hear of some new connection between oral and overall health, the latest linking perio disease and Alzheimer's. But people continue to smoke, eat low-nutrition food, and not save money for retirement simply because they don't consider the long-term effects of their actions.

So how do you do change this? Education? I'm going to take a radical view on this and say, "No." At least not at the outset. People already know they should eat right and save money. But we are 40 percent obese and only 3 percent of the population retires financially secure. I suggest that education comes second. Remember your favorite teacher in high school? Didn't you learn the most in that class? Same concept.

> **Having a remarkable dental practice opens people's minds to a long-term view of their oral health.**

Which brings me back to the idea that dentistry is subjective. It *starts* with the experience of being in your dental practice. It begins with the practice atmosphere, the attitude of your team, the design of your office. I am convinced that having a great dental practice is what opens people's minds to a long-term view of their oral health, not some brilliant explanation.

The most successful dentists I know have high treatment acceptance not because they educate their patients extremely well. Many times patients don't know much at all about the treatment itself (or don't even *want* to know). But they like their dentist. In fact, they *really* like her. They trust her. They like going to her office. They like the people who work there.

And here's something else: They get the sense that everyone in the practice genuinely cares about them. As human beings, not just as patients. And not just as a source of income.

So if we really want to help patients, we have to understand their psychology and accept that we need to persuade them that their teeth are important. We can't always come at the problem directly. And realize that by creating an environment that is fun, comfortable, convenient, and filled with compassionate people, we open their minds—and their hearts—to taking care of their teeth. And that lays the foundation for the second step, educating them.

And let's not forget that social media has become an excellent way for you to demonstrate what the experience of your dental practice is like and for your patients to do it as well. Comments on Facebook, photos of happy patients, video testimonials, and online reviews are all essentially revolutionary ways that people can discover what it's like to be a patient of yours.

The general population sees dentistry as something that can easily be avoided or ignored, and that their teeth don't have to be straight, their gums can bleed ("That's normal, right?"), and their breath can be disgusting. But we know better. And knowing better hasn't done us much good. We're a lot like life insurance salesmen, trying to get people to think long term *and* about something unpleasant at the same time. Tough combination.

So let's try a different approach. Outsmart people for their own good, and offer them a dental practice they can't resist. Hey, it might be kind of fun to work at a place like that, too!

CHAPTER 11

BEING WORTHY
OF TRUST

There is a terrific book on prioritizing your actions called *The One Thing* by Gary Keller, which I highly recommend. It presents a precise question that you can use to clarify your priorities. And I'll ask it to you:

What is the *one thing* that you could do in your practice that would make everything else you do easier or not necessary?

It's a big question. Is it to have great advertising that attracts tons of new patients? No, because that makes a lot of things harder, especially if you don't give a great patient experience. Is it answering the phone well at the front desk? That certainly is critical, but it doesn't make everything else easier, just some things.

This is my answer: Build trust.

And here's why:

- They will accept comprehensive treatment because they trust you.
- They will spend beyond their insurance because they trust you.
- They will be consistent in recall because they trust you.
- They will recommend you because they trust you.

So how do you build trust? Trust is a wall built brick by brick. Action by action. A wall without holes. Without cracks. Which means they shouldn't be able to see through it and see an ulterior motive.

Show them that you care about them as people, not patients. Know who they are, what their concerns are, what their interests are. Listen to them, relate to them, interact with them as people. Don't judge them. Don't scold them. Ask questions about what matters to them. Understand their financial situation and accommodate that. Check in with them in the evening to see how their treatment recovery is going.

Trust is a wall built brick by brick. They shouldn't be able to see through it and see an ulterior motive.

That patient you are trying to convince to take care of his teeth is the same man who gets talked into doing repairs on his car. He knows that the dealership wants to make money, but he also wants to drive a safe vehicle and wants it to last as long as possible. So he weighs his options. Does he trust the service advisor? He does if he knows him and the man has been fair with him before this. It's a simple formula: Once money and unknowable conditions are factors, the less relationship, the more distrust.

Let's say you have a nail in your tire and take it to a tire repair center. If the mechanic took the nail out and said, "This tire doesn't need to be replaced now, but if it happens again it will," you'd suddenly trust him a lot more. And then if the next time it happens, he said, "This tire can't be saved. I can't in good conscience let you drive on it if I just patch it," you'd believe him and buy a new tire.

Did you really know for certain that you needed a new tire? No. Trust is not knowledge, but a substitute for knowledge when we don't have it.

If you're looking for guidelines on how to build trust, here are three:

Integrity trumps profit. This means your actions clearly show that you are going to do the right thing for that other person, regardless of your potential gain. It's not always easy, but it makes decisions on what you and your team should do in any given situation very easy. Act accordingly and accept the consequences. Because nothing destroys trust more than when money trumps integrity.

Your reputation is a reverberation of your trustworthiness. In other words, the first layer of trust is being built by what other patients say about you, not by a direct experience of you and your practice. You are your brand, and you need to be a trusted brand to succeed in the long run.

Know your audience. Different people grant trust in different ways, for different reasons. The better you are at understanding who you're talking to, who this person is and how they make decisions, the faster you will be able to build trust. So that's what the next two chapters will be about.

CHAPTER 12

THE ETLID
FALLACY

As I mentioned in the last chapter, part of building trust is understanding the person you're talking to. There are three facets to this: what their demographic information is, how they like to communicate from a personality standpoint, and what generation they are from. But foundational to that understanding is to let go of your own biases.

What do you suppose is the biggest blunder made in practice marketing? Is it not answering the phone properly? Or not tracking your advertising results? Perhaps not having a good, dynamic website? Nope. Those are all up there, but the biggest marketing mistake that business owners make is *assuming that everyone thinks like you do.*

This is the ETLID Fallacy. (Everyone Thinks Like **I** **D**o).

The biggest marketing mistake business owners make is assuming that everyone thinks like they do.

Why is that so bad? Because it influences all the other marketing and advertising decisions, and it's not based on factual, statistical data about consumer behavior. I hear these opinions all the time from dentists and, to a lesser degree, office managers. Things like, "I believe in calling all our patients rather than texting them. It's more personal," or "People are tired of surveys."

What the person saying this means is that *he feels* phone calls are more personal than texting, or *she* is tired of surveys, and therefore everyone is. The reality is that 30 percent of people who use texting *prefer* it to a phone call.[5] So they don't find a phone call personal, they find it annoying. And when it comes to surveys and reviews, if you were to get 1 out of 20 people to respond, that is an excellent result and will boost your SEO considerably. So what if some people have "survey fatigue?" Should you not do them? Of course not.

> **Be realistic about your demographics, and do your homework before you move to a new location or a new city.**

Dentists are essentially scientists, making decisions more analytically than the average person. But don't kid yourself. You yourself are influenced by subconscious inclinations more than you even know.

In the early years of 1-800-DENTIST, I would have dentists telling me what TV shows I should be advertising on. This was based on the shows that they liked to watch. Instead, I used the statistical data that told me which shows got the most response and the best quality of patient. Call me crazy. I never watched an entire episode of *Oprah*, but she got several million dollars from us over the years. Why? Because I didn't use my personal preferences, I used results based on research.

I don't mean to sound all high and mighty about this. It's a reflex response. I recently spoke to the dental students at Harvard, and one student remarked, "I'm not attracted to all that personal stuff companies post on Facebook business pages. It seems frivolous and irrelevant." She may be right about that with regard to many other businesses, but the fact is many people are looking for exactly that on a dental practice's Facebook page, because the experience of being a patient is what influences them to go, stay, and accept treatment, not clinical skills. Conversely, show them a video of your best crown prep and they're gone.

We all tend to make these ETLID assumptions, and we're wrong way more than we're right. On your road to remarkable, I want you to catch yourself when you do it, and try to find out what's really true whenever possible.

SOME OTHER CLASSIC ETLID ASSUMPTIONS:

"Facebook is kid stuff." The fact is that the largest group of Facebook users is 35-54, and the fastest-growing group of Facebook users is the over-55 population.[6]

"People don't care about design when it comes to spending." Really? Look at the pricing difference between Dunkin

Donuts® and Starbucks®, or Apple versus Dell®, and tell me if that opinion passes the reality check. We spend based on packaging, and that goes for your dental office just as much as a bottle of Grey Goose®.

"My patients don't use email." Wrong. Ninety-seven percent of Americans have email, and over 90 percent check it every day.[7]

"No one is going to choose a dentist on Facebook." Except that 25 percent of Facebook users said they would be willing to find a dentist that way.[8]

"My patients love me." Some do, for sure. But when we used our live operators to call dormant patients for practices, how is it that 50 percent of their "dormant" patients had changed to another dentist? And only a quarter of those are people who have moved away. Somebody didn't love their dentist. But they're not going to call and tell the practice they're leaving.

"Website design doesn't matter as much as content." Just the opposite. Research has shown that consumers are making judgments about your clinical skills based on the *appearance* of your website. I know that those two things are unrelated. And in this example is another important point: Many times those ETLID opinions are based on logic or reasonable assumptions. The truth is that consumers don't always act rationally or logically, especially when it comes to dentistry.

"People are flakes when it comes to keeping their dental appointments." Okay, this one is true.

It isn't just small business owners who make this mistake. I know executives at very large organizations making the same sort of "gut" decisions and putting millions of dollars behind them. With the same poor results.

Statistics tell you what most people do. I've been doing advertising long enough to stop trying to figure out why. I just go with the data. I accept that people act irrationally and that most people don't think the way I do about most things. And the numbers tell me that website design matters, social media is important, digital communication is the new norm, reviews influence consumers, and everything a patient experiences in the practice influences their acceptance of treatment.

Valuable data is easier to access than ever. Use it to balance your opinion. Hey, you may even be right sometimes. But the reality is, everyone doesn't think like you do.

So let's get into who your patients are.

CHAPTER 13

KNOW YOUR
DEMOGRAPHIC

Every neighborhood is different, and every neighborhood is evolving. It is either gentrifying, aging, or degrading. And always at different speeds.

You might say that you want to practice in a city like Beverly Hills. First of all, in that area there is a dentist for every 278 residents. Not good. Second, dentists I know with practices in Beverly Hills say that when you encounter old money there, they still want the same prices they paid in the '60s. Not good. And what is your rent going to be? How about patient parking?

There are deep questions you need to know about your practice, so you can anticipate trends. The key ones are:

- What are the key businesses in the area with good dental plans? Are they stable?
- What are the dominant ethnicities? What is their social attitude toward dental health?

- Is there a major second language being spoken?
- What direction have house prices been going over the past 10 years?
- How many people have children?
- How many are retired?
- What's the median income?
- What's the unemployment rate?
- How many dentists are there per household?

Then you want to know what the traffic is like near your future office, who will see your signage if you have it, and what usual and customary fees are.

If you are in an established practice, this information is still valuable. If another ethnicity is starting to dominate, that will determine who your best associate candidate would be. Which businesses are moving in, and which are moving out? What are their dental plans? Is the population aging or refreshing itself?

If your demographics are spiraling downward, don't just wait until the neighborhood is completely turned. Move! You want a practice that's worth selling when you finally retire, don't you? It's never too late to start over in a dental practice. I've seen it done at every age. But there reaches a point where hoping for things to improve in your neighborhood, despite a steady trend indicating the opposite, is basically like waiting for the rotary phone to make a comeback. Or pen pals.

I know practices in Florida that depended on NASA, and whose entire patient base lost their jobs and their dental coverage in a single year. That can be nearly fatal for a practice. However, most of the time these shifts happen gradually, and the practice keeps eroding until you find yourself moving closer and closer to not escaping gravity every month as you shrink. Then you start making bad decisions. Cutting marketing, cutting hygiene hours, cutting back on investments in technology and training, not bonusing the team. I call these choices the frostbite of dentistry. The body is shutting down heat and sacrificing extremities to stay alive. Not a growth plan. And often not a survival one.

Evolve or die. Be realistic about your demographics, and do your homework before you move to a new location or a new city.

> **Cutting back on marketing and advertising is business frostbite.**

There is still abundance in this profession, but you have to know where the patients are, and who you intend to serve. There are perfectly good business models for offering basic triage care to low-income patients, and obviously they are necessary. But you would be severely impairing your odds if you tried to do a fee-for-service practice in the same neighborhood.

Often it's a matter of striking a happy medium. An acquaintance of mine, upon hearing what I did for a living, said, "I'm looking for a great dentist with low overhead." A very telling remark. Sounds like he's looking for faster, better, and cheaper. And I don't think he's alone. So once you decide the audience you want to serve, create your business around the needs of that demographic, and strive to give them all three.

Once you understand the nature of your practice demographics, you need to deepen your understanding on an individual patient level in order to effectively build a relationship as a trusted advisor. In particular, you need to learn how they view dentistry. That comes down to these four main questions:

HOW DO THEY VALUE DENTISTRY?

In other words, how important is their oral health to them? Does their smile relate to their work? Do they see a connection between their overall health and their oral health? Probe this first, as it will guide you as to how far you have to bring this person to get them to value dentistry appropriately.

WHAT HAS BEEN THEIR EXPERIENCE OF DENTISTRY SO FAR?

Did they have a dentist previously that they loved and trusted? Or was it the opposite experience? Did they feel cared for? That they were well informed on how to maintain their teeth? Are they hoping for the same experience or something better? What didn't they like about their previous dental experiences?

WHAT IS THEIR FINANCIAL SITUATION?

Are they employed? Well employed? Do they need financing? (Often their answer will include their creditworthiness.) Dental insurance is part of their financial picture. How do they view their dental coverage? Do they see it as something that dictates care or just a discount plan? This is critical to assess, as you will have to move them to an accurate understanding of dental coverage very early on in the relationship.

WHERE DO THEY FIT ON THE EMOTIONAL/ANALYTICAL SPECTRUM?

Are they frightened about dental treatment? Does cost make them anxious? Does the treatment? Do they respond to the friendliness of the team or not seem to care? Do they want detailed explanations of the procedure? Are they fascinated by the new technology or could care less? We all fit somewhere on this spectrum, and the better you can assess that about the patient, the more effective your communication will be. Someone who is extremely anxious is not going to process information well, so your goal will be to say things that will calm and reassure him. Another may want to know the long-term viability of your bonding agents. Each patient is experiencing you and your practice differently. Being tuned in to their needs and where they fit on this spectrum will yield significantly better results in case presentation.

Obviously there is a great deal more to case presentation, and there are some excellent teachers out there who know way more than I do about it. But this will give you a strong foundation to build a long relationship, based upon trust and empathy.

CHAPTER 14

CROSSING THE
DIGITAL DIVIDE

As you endeavor to understand your patients better, know this: You are now dealing with four different generations of patients (five, if you do ortho or pedodontics). They all behave quite differently, and you need to modify your practice behavior accordingly. By the way, these generational differences apply to your team members as well.

Here is how the current generations break out in terms of age and population:

Matures: Born before 1945; 29 million
Baby Boomers: Born between 1945 and1965; 75 million
Gen X: Born between 1966 and 1981; 66 million
Millennials: Born between 1982 and 2001; 75 million
Gen Z: Born after 2001

Matures behave in what I would describe as a traditional way. This means essentially that they are brand loyal, respond to traditional types of advertising, and maintain a smaller network of friends. They communicate by telephone or face to face. Except for this: According to a Pew Research study, 43 percent of seniors who are on the web use social media.[9] And that was in 2013.

Baby Boomers have ruled the economy for decades and in some ways still do. But they are migrating out of the workforce and into retirement. They are also inheriting the largest transfer of wealth in the history of mankind as their parents pass away. They live longer and have enjoyed the steady modernization of the world, but it has impacted their later careers in a significant way. Brand loyalty is diminishing. But they have come to expect technology to improve their life instead of just complicate it, particularly when it comes to their health. They are a generation not comfortable with the prospect of aging and spend accordingly.

Generation X has grown up in a world that was computerizing but had not yet become connected. Careers became less predictable, education less reliable or useful, politics more disturbing than ever. Boomers remember the day JFK was shot, Gen-X remembers Nixon resigning. They've lived through three recessions, including the Dot Com bust. In short, they were forced to be adaptable, learning new careers, migrating to the Sun Belt in greater numbers, and they grew up being less optimistic about their economic prospects. They are growing in concern about their health, but work is the main priority.

Millennials, also called, Generation Y, have had the Internet for their entire lives. Most have had mobile phones since they were early teens. They live on social media, sharing constantly, and take photos of everything they eat, see, and do. They date people they met online and they break up with them with a text. Their world is an "on demand" world, where almost anything they want can be found or acquired with a phone app—from a car ride, to an apartment for rent, to a place to have Chinese food at 2am. Digital technology is woven into every fabric of their lives. The accelerating pace of change is normal to them. They will likely live to over 100 years old, but have barely begun to care about their long-term health.

Be very mindful of this fact: Millennials became the largest generation in the workforce in 2015, over 35 percent, as the Baby Boomers move into retirement. They just passed Generation X in total numbers and by 2025, they will be 75 percent of the workforce. Clearly, they will also become a major part of your patient base.

Some other facts about Millennials:

- They are much less loyal to brands and companies than Boomers.
- They will change jobs and even careers much more than the older generations did.
- They have children later.
- They spend less time watching television than they do online.

THE DIGITAL DIVIDE

But remember, much as there is a distinction between generations, the real separation is between someone who is connected and someone who isn't, regardless of their age. Once someone adapts to the Internet, crossing the Digital Divide, as I call it, then their behavior will mimic the Millennials, even if they are older.

So what does a Connected Person want?

- 24-hour access to information
- Peer assessments of businesses—online reviews and social media posts
- Everything about a business available through a website or social media
- Minimal steps to acquire information
- Decreasing direct human contact
- Everything faster—information, deliveries, responses
- Ever-changing, ever-improving technology
- Convenience at an ever-increasing level

You will need to communicate differently with the Connected. You will need to market and promote yourself differently. You as a team will still need to straddle the digital divide to satisfy every generation in your patient base. But keep your focus on what the Connected Person wants.

CHAPTER 15

SOCIAL MEDIA IS CHANGING HUMAN BEHAVIOR

The digital revolution has turned into the digital evolution. We are now in a constant state of change and adaptation. Much of this is driven by social media. In the past year, Facebook has gone from being predominantly images to an ever-increasing number of videos being uploaded. And they start playing automatically as you scroll down to them on your wall. In fact, Facebook now has more of the highest-volume-viewed videos than YouTube®, all because of the tendency people have to share what they've watched much more on Facebook.

One out of five Internet visits is to Facebook.[10] And people find Facebook recommendations three times more trustworthy than Yelp reviews. And only slightly less than word of mouth. Why? It's because people think they are from their friends, or at least friends of friends.

With respect to your dental practice, having a Facebook presence has gone from not possible to silly to essential over the course of eight years. Earlier I mentioned a recent survey, which showed that 25 percent of Facebook users would be comfortable finding a dentist through the site. Think about how fast that happened. And, of course, that percentage will be even higher for Millennials.

The beauty of all these changes in media is that as you become a remarkable practice, the world will know. You will have to be fully engaged in the online world to fully leverage the benefits of social media, but the opportunity is unlike anything that has ever existed for businesses.

The other dimension that has changed all of business is the online review world. In some ways I consider this a part of social media, because it is people sharing opinions about their experiences with products and services. But it deserves its own section, which follows.

CHAPTER 16

RANDOM IDIOTIC OPINIONS

This is the reality of today's digital world. A complete stranger can post a review of your business—anonymously—and have it appear as part of the listing of your practice on that review website. It's permanent, will come up in a search, and can only be removed by the anonymous poster.

You can rail about how unfair this is all day long. But it is the reality, and it's not going away. In fact, the opposite is happening. Consumer use of reviews is on the constant rise. The Connected Generation believes in reading and posting reviews and gives them great credence.

How did this happen? For a long time, reviews were a territory reserved for established, prestigious entities like *The New York Times Review of Books*, the *Zagat® Travel Guide*, or Siskel & Ebert. Then Amazon changed everything. Their website started to allow the public to review books. And no matter what people said about a book, Amazon would leave the review up.

The major book publishers were up in arms: "How can you allow people to write bad reviews about our books? That's bad for business!" they cried. Amazon didn't care. They brought reviewing to the masses and gave everyone a voice.

Shortly thereafter, TripAdvisor® came along and let people review hotels, vacation spots, and restaurants. And Rotten Tomatoes™ (now Flickr®) let the audience review movies. And people read them. Then along came Yelp. And, of course, there is the mother of all review sites, Google (who, coincidentally, bought Zagat and added its reviews to their own). It turns out, people don't really care what the experts have to say anywhere near as much as they like what I call RIOs (Random Idiotic Opinions). They like to read several reviews and see for themselves what the public thinks. It doesn't seem to matter much at all how educated, well-informed or articulate these anonymous reviewers are.

An ever-increasing number of people will not buy something or use a service without reading a review first. And if they can't find reviews about that business, they move on to one that does have reviews. It's become a huge industry. Yelp alone is worth around $3 billion. So don't spend much time waiting for this trend to blow over. If anything, it will continue to expand as more and more people use smart phones for everything. (According to Google's Multi-Screen World Study in 2014, 61 percent of online searches start on a mobile device. Wow.)

So why are reviews so popular? I believe it's just human nature. When we didn't know about something, we asked someone. Sometimes it would be a friend, but often it was a complete stranger. Imagine if 10 years ago you walked into a store, looked at a TV, and then could ask 30 people who already owned one what they liked or didn't like about it. Why wouldn't you do that? You'd weigh each opinion differently, maybe, but you wouldn't really care what the IQ was of each person telling you. Today that's called turning on your smart phone. It's just too easy. And you see people doing precisely that in Best Buy every day.

There is a negative side to this level of public freedom of expression. We live in a new world, but it's not a brave new world—it's more like a cowardly one. People feel very empowered using the Internet to vent about a business or even carry out personal vendettas. They can attack virtually anonymously, with impunity. (The court dockets are full of failed attempts at suing Yelp and/or negative reviewers.) The reality is, it's almost impossible to get a negative review down.

There is also a whole new industry of writing fake positive reviews. A recent Harvard study estimated that 20 percent of online reviews are fake.[11] Twenty percent! Most are written by shadowy businesses, usually in foreign countries, whose only job is to pump up someone's business and get paid for doing it. There's even a term for it: *astroturfing*. Some government agencies are starting to crack down on businesses paying for this, but it's going to take some time to make a dent in that 20 percent.

On the other hand, if you're a remarkable dentist, this whole online review thing is a fabulous opportunity for free promotion. You can turn reviews to your advantage in two major ways. First, people do give them credence, and millions of people have chosen a dentist based on Yelp or Google reviews. So if you have a steady stream of great reviews, you have built a terrific online reputation for yourself. Second, those reviews will boost your search engine optimization (SEO), because Google looks at reviews as one of the elements it uses to determine your website's relevance in a search.

You need a systematic strategy for generating a steady stream of online reviews.

So what can you do? The short answer is you need a systematic strategy for generating a steady stream of reviews on Google and Yelp, and someone on your team dedicated to monitoring and responding to reviews. The long answer is in *Everything is Marketing,* but I also repeat it in *Appendix II,* as it is so important to have the right approach.

CHAPTER 17

IS SELLING
UNPROFESSIONAL?

A remarkable dental practice loves to sell dentistry. *Loves* it. Because the whole team knows in their hearts that dentistry is one of the best investments a person can make, and that most people don't realize that.

But isn't selling unprofessional? Not at all, despite what you may have heard from your professors in school or various society board members, or even your peers. In fact, I think it's more unprofessional NOT to sell dentistry.

Why? Isn't selling some vile, despicable process where people get talked into something they don't need and can't afford?

Not exactly. Selling is just communication with a purpose. It is neither negative nor positive. In reality, we sell all the time, but just don't call it that.

When I use the term selling, what I mean is communication with a purpose, that purpose in this case being the acceptance of treatment that is in the best interest of the patient. I think a lot of dentists have a negative attitude toward the concept of selling exactly because they have been told, erroneously, that it is unprofessional to do so. But when someone doesn't understand the value of something, the advantages of something, and the benefit to themselves, they require information, and often persuasion, to make a decision that's beneficial to them. I emphasized in my first book that when you have something good to sell, that is to the user's benefit—not just yours—then that is a positive thing. And because the typical patient doesn't appreciate their need or understand the value of dentistry, they need to be effectively persuaded to do something for their own good, and their own good health.

I had an insight recently about human nature and people's behavior with regard to dental treatment, which was this: *People don't have buyer's remorse when it comes to dentistry.* Think about it. When's the last time a patient came back and said, "I wish I hadn't gotten these implants and was still eating baby food," or, "I wish I hadn't blown that money on that root canal and my jaw was still throbbing insanely." It doesn't happen.

> ## People don't have buyer's remorse when it comes to dentistry.

People have buyer's remorse with all sorts of things they spend money on: electronics, clothes, cars, even houses. But they don't have it with dentistry. This to me is the strongest indicator of the real value of what you do. I sincerely believe that if you encounter a patient who is in need of restorative dentistry for both the quality of their life and the maintenance of their health, then you are being unprofessional by not making your best effort to persuade them to undergo treatment. Why? Because the primary beneficiary of the treatments is the patient, not you.

And that's critical to remember. Of course you will be paid to do the treatment. But it's not about you getting rich, it's about them getting healthier. Most patients are woefully ignorant about the importance of oral health. Or the downside of delaying treatment. Help them.

And that's the basic formula: If something is valuable, critical to the health and well-being of a person, and also largely misunderstood, you have something that needs to be sold.

Sure, it would be great if people wanted the maximum dentistry they could get, as fast as possible. But they don't. They think putting it off has no consequences. Which is part of why it's your responsibility to facilitate that treatment acceptance with effective presentation and persuasion skills.

Most people need to be talked into getting life insurance. Is it a bad thing to have? Quite the opposite. But like dentistry, not a lot of fun is associated with the expenditure. And saving for retirement is by definition a delaying of gratification, which is why I have to twist my employees' arms to put some money into their 401(k). Am I a cheap hustler for doing it? Or am I helping them to take a longer view of life than the next two weeks?

That's the challenge of dentistry, too—the fact that it's about a long-term investment, which most people don't find appealing, especially when instant gratification is everywhere else. All the more reason to refine your presentation skills, not just your clinical ones, remembering that all important maxim that value is a perception, not a calculation.

I sell all the time, and I'm proud of it, because I know that what I'm offering helps dentists to succeed. And I also know that most of the time they would much rather spend their money on something more fun, like a new laser or a Maserati®, but my persuasive skills help them to take the long view about building their business. I would consider myself unprofessional if I didn't convince a dentist who had no website that it was high time he got one, or if I let an office manager continue to believe that her patients don't want reminders by text, when I know that half of them do.

Will I make money in the process? Yes. There's no crime, no shame in win/win. My simple goal is that their benefit is greater than mine. As long as my core value—integrity trumps profit—guides us, then I want my team to get better and better at selling.

If you're reluctant to develop your sales skills, then I adamantly maintain that you are doing your patients a disservice.

In relationships, I have a guiding principle that I use. I ask myself, what is the most loving thing to do for this person at this moment? And it applies to business too, and especially dentistry, which requires more tough love than a lot of other life situations. Is it *loving* to let a patient think that putting off treatment will not have negative repercussions? Is it *loving* to leave them ignorant of the need and benefits of treatment? No. It's just easier. Less stressful. And irresponsible, I believe.

If you're reluctant to develop your sales skills, then I adamantly maintain that you are doing your patients a disservice. And if you don't have team members who not only believe in the value of dentistry but are comfortable convincing patients to accept treatment, then they are also doing your patients a disservice.

Patients come to you as the professional. Fulfill that role.

SECTION THREE:

CREATING THE REMARKABLE ENVIRONMENT

REMARKABLE DENTIST #2

Craig Spodak, DMD
Spodak Dental Group
Delray Beach, FL
spodakdental.com
facebook.com/spodakdental

Year opened: 1976

REMARKABLE NUMBERS:

Associates: 9
Annual revenue:
For the 8 years prior to 2006, less than $900,000;
By 2009, it reached $2.4 million;
In the first year of the new facility, $7.4 million.
Dr. Spodak is a third generation dentist.
New office square footage: 13,000
Spodak Dental is an Invisalign® Super Elite Practice
   (top 1 percent in the world in case starts)

REMARKABLE TECHNOLOGIES:

CEREC, GALILEOS™, digital radiography, lasers
His new building is a LEED Gold Certified Facility

REMARKABLE BEHAVIOR:

Believing that vertical integration—having all dental services available in one facility—was the way of the future, Craig Spodak took a bold, serious risk and built a brand new 13,000 square foot practice, filled with natural light, open space, and digital technology.

His idea was to combine an amazing facility with an amazing team, resulting in an unparalleled patient experience. But as he was about to open the doors of his new facility, Craig sat in his office with his head in his hands, muttering to himself, "What have I done?"

His father, also a dentist, came in and told his son not to worry, reassuring him that no matter what, they would work together to make the practice a success. The first year of revenue proved his father right.

The practice currently has six general dentists and four specialists and, despite having a large business to run, Dr. Spodak still does dentistry five days a week.

In building a team, Dr. Spodak doesn't just focus on motivated, capable people, but is looking for people actively engaged in social media. Team members are encouraged rather than prohibited from posting during work hours.

Spodak Dental accepts most insurance plans. Years earlier Dr. Spodak had experimented with dropping all his plans, and it arrested his practice growth. Lesson learned.

Lastly, they have massaging operatory chairs.

REMARKABLE QUOTE:

"When you have an unhappy patient, that's the greatest opportunity to be remarkable."

WHAT PEOPLE SAY:

"It was a comforting and honest experience. I could say it was wonderful, but talking about dentistry and wonder might seem far-fetched. However, it was wonderful. I was treated with kindness, respect, and it did not feel as if I was being sold a bag of goods. Everyone I met was pleasant and courteous without being over the top. The grounds and the space itself were beautiful and inspiring. I went in for a consult and left with a new dentist after being with the same one for 16 years. Thanks, Spodak!"

"Whenever I go to Spodak Dental it feels like I am the most important person there. I have someone greet me, take me to the back, ask me if I want refreshments, and their chairs can give you a massage! The staff is extremely professional and friendly. Dr. Patel took her time on my first visit to give me my cleaning, which is unheard of to me. She was extremely diligent and answered all of my questions regarding my concerns over continued care of my teeth. I am totally recommending this place to all of my friends and family."

"LOVE IT! Every time has been great. The friendliest facility I've ever been to. Happy staff, wonderful equipment. They're not afraid to take the time to talk to you, and the atmosphere is much nicer. Their bigger rooms with window views really strip away the awkward office feeling I get at most dental facilities. I'm telling everyone about this place!"

CHAPTER 18

YOUR PRACTICE
IS TOO SMALL

Yes, that's right.

It's too small to have someone less than fantastic at the front desk.

It's too small to avoid being on Facebook.

It's too small to not have convenient hours.

It's too small to ignore the competition.

It's too small to not sign your own checks.

It's too small to ignore online reviews.

It's too small to not give every new patient a tour of the office.

It's too small to have any employees who don't have a great attitude.

It's too small for the dentist not to do personal welcome calls to all new patients.

It's too small to let any call go to voicemail.

It's too small to not ask each of your patients for referrals.

It's too small to not have a great website.

And no matter how big your practice gets, these will all still be true. That is, if you want to create a remarkable practice.

CHAPTER 19

KNOW YOUR WHY

SIX ASPECTS OF A REMARKABLE DENTAL PRACTICE

Simply put, these are the spokes of the remarkable wheel. They are essential, interdependent, and are true for the practice, the dentists, and the team members.

- Trustworthy
- Genuinely cares about patients
- Technologically advanced
- Clinically excellent
- Grateful
- Patient-centric

Most are self-explanatory, and we'll build on them in the coming chapters, but let me give more color to the concept of being a patient-centric practice. It means you ask that most basic question: What does your patient really want? The remarkable dental practice cares about this and makes every effort to provide solutions. And sometimes it's what they want on the surface—comfort, low cost, speed, convenience, financing, a pleasant atmosphere, and happy people—and other times it's the deeper thing, which is to be healed, taken out of pain, made beautiful, or made able to eat again.

There is no better way to sharpen your focus than by asking, whenever you're making a decision about anything from an office policy to a technology purchase, "Does this help us give the patients what they want?"

Which brings us to the discussion of why you do dentistry.

DISCOVERING YOUR WHY

The most important thing you can do in your practice is to know why you are doing what you're doing. As I mentioned earlier, I am greatly inspired by the author Simon Sinek, and he is adamant that any great business, any business that wants to continue to thrive in a world of accelerating change, has to know it's WHY (and I'll keep capitalizing it as he does in his book, *Start with Why*).

You should certainly have practice goals. You should have a vision statement. But at the core of that is understanding your purpose, the real reason you're doing dentistry every day. This in some ways is a very personal thing. We all have different things that motivate us and give us purpose, but for most dentists, I'm guessing (and hoping) you're not doing it just to get rich. I'm pretty sure you also like helping people and making them healthy.

This purpose needs to be precisely defined so that you can clearly express it, not just directly with your patients, although that is critical and where it starts, but in all of your communication and marketing. And it guides you with building your team as well. When they know your WHY, and you find people with that same WHY, you are unstoppable.

Not every business does this. And not every business stays true to its WHY. Apple knows its WHY, which is to challenge conventional thinking in every category of business it tackles. And it does it over and over again. Kodak forgot its WHY. It was in the photo sharing business and it thought it was in the film business. When Sam Walton started Walmart, his WHY was to serve people—his employees, customers, and the community. But once he was gone, the company lost its purpose and became convinced its WHY was to be cheap. And it didn't just forget about its employees, it neglected them. The Walmart of today faces countless class action lawsuits related to wage violations and gender discrimination. It even trains its new employees how to apply for food stamps. I don't consider that serving people, and I don't think Sam would either.

Over time, companies drift away from their WHY and get more concerned with *how* they do something, and they focus on doing that better. That's not so much wrong as misguided, because the truth is that they've lost their way. Your WHY is your guiding light through every year and every decision.

So how do you get to your WHY and clearly define it? The idea is to really get to the heart of the matter. And to keep it simple. The best way to understand is to see the process of someone getting to it. This is a conversation I had with a dentist helping her define her WHY.

ME: So, Karen, tell me what gives you the most satisfaction about being a dentist.

KAREN: Well, I really love working with my hands. The surgery I do every day excites me.

ME: That's great. And is that what gets you out of bed in the morning?

KAREN: I'd have to say that what really motivates me is coming here and working with my team. They're awesome.

ME: So that's a big part of it.

KAREN: And our patients really respond to them. It allows me to do a lot of dentistry. It motivates me to get better.

ME: Sounds nice. But why do you find all this so satisfying?

KAREN: I guess it's because I'm helping people get healthier. Often in spite of themselves. (She laughs.)

ME: Aha. So it's not just working with your hands or working with your team. It's that you're helping people.

KAREN: That's really who I am. I'm someone who cares about getting people healthy. My skill is in dentistry, but it's fulfilling because I know that my patients' lives are better because of what we do.

ME: So if you had a guiding principle for your practice, would it be helping people get healthier?

KAREN: Absolutely. That's what really makes it all worthwhile for me.

ME: Then that's your "WHY," Karen. And it's a good one.

I hope that your WHY is something close to this: "Helping people get healthier." Do you see what that encompasses? It goes beyond "delivering excellent dentistry every day." That is certainly a desirable goal, but it narrows your focus to what you do, rather than who you serve. It's not why you do it, but rather what you're doing because of some specific WHY.

I think my dentist friend's most accurate definition is how she put it: "Helping people get healthier, often in spite of themselves." It encompasses the entire breadth of being a remarkable dentist (which she is, of course!): great skills, great team, great attitude, while also knowing that you have to give patients a great experience so that they will accept the dentistry that will make them healthier.

Knowing and acting on your WHY builds trust. In fact, it's the foundation of trust. Your WHY is your foundational belief, your *how* is the actions you take based on that belief, and your *what* is the result of those actions. Your patients first need to feel your WHY, and once they do they will start to trust you.

And the more they experience your WHY from your team, the more that trust grows.

On the other hand, if your only WHY is to make a lot of money, you are going to find that increasingly problematic. How much money is enough? What exactly are you hoping to buy or do with that money? Stop doing dentistry? Then you have no WHY at all to get you to show up. You can't build trust, you can't inspire team members, and you will eventually be miserable, and that will destroy your practice.

I know dentists who make an incredibly good living. And their practice grows every year and their patients love and trust them. Some of them even drive a Ferrari® to work (though I don't recommend it!). Isn't this a dentist whose purpose is making a lot of money? Nope. Money is simply one of the results. It is not the driving force, the guiding principle. It's what happens when you do everything right and you know why you're really doing it.

What happens when your purpose for doing dentistry shifts from making people healthy to making money? Patients will eventually sense that. Many dentists experience this change in the course of their career. Simon Sinek calls it "the split," when your practice moves away from its higher purpose—helping people—and money moves up to first position. I'll say this with utter conviction from 40 years of being in business: when that happens, you are sunk. Not right away. It's a slow death, like you started smoking three packs a day. But until you recognize it as the cancer that will be your practice's demise, and dig down deep and find your way back to your true purpose, no marketing, no tricks, no consultants can save you. If as the dentist you're at that point, or you're beyond the "split," when all you worry about is how much more money you can make, then you need to take serious action.

Look at the list below. If more than one or two of these are true for you, you've drifted away from an inspiring purpose:

1. When you have a great month, you buy yourself something expensive, and no one gets a bonus.
2. You complain about how much you pay in taxes and how everyone else is leeching off you.
3. You make more than you've ever made, but you worry about money more than ever.
4. You're annoyed with how ignorant patients are.
5. You resent patients who don't accept treatment.

When you understand your WHY, a lot falls into place, and you're well on your way to becoming remarkable. Take the time to clearly define that for yourself, and if you are a team member, make sure you are in a practice that aligns with your personal and professional WHY.

When you establish your WHY, several beliefs flow directly from it. These are what I see as guiding principles for a practice.

GUIDING PRINCIPLES OF A REMARKABLE DENTAL TEAM

- Fun is essential, fun is contagious.
- Appreciation needs to be expressed, an environment of thankfulness cultivated.
- Technology is an investment, essential to providing ever-better care.
- Dentistry needs to be sold to patients.
- Abundance is the reality you create, leading to generosity, contribution, and optimism.
- Patient experience is paramount.
- Dentistry is one of the best long-term investments a person can make.
- Everything is a team effort.

All of these contribute to the creation of a great team. All of these lead to profit. But what they lead to most is a fulfilling, gratifying career.

One more thing: Being remarkable is a heck of a lot more fun than just grinding out basic dentistry every day, like a tooth repair shop. So let's talk about how to get there.

CHAPTER 20

A GOAL WITHOUT
A PLAN IS A WISH

Once you understand your WHY, it will be important for the practice to have clear, achievable, ambitious goals. Note those three adjectives, as they are the essential elements of any goal. First, be *clear* about each goal. If it is a monthly production number, or a percentage of growth over the previous month, spell it out so that the whole team knows exactly what you're going for. It has to be *achievable*, meaning the team believes you can get there, but it should also be *ambitious*, pushing everyone to a new boundary.

And then it needs to be written down, and everyone needs to commit to it. Most consultants recommend you operate with three production goals: a daily goal, a monthly one, and an annual one. From a marketing standpoint, I might add two more: a goal for new patients per month and a recall goal.

So your practice goals might look like this:

- Annual production: 20 percent increase over the previous year. It can be a dollar amount or a percentage, and it will determine your daily and monthly goals.
- January production goal: $60,000. This should increase with each month to reach the annual goal.
- Daily production goal for January (20 practice days): $3,000.
- Monthly new patient goal for January: 45.
- Recall goal: Improve average recall for active patients from 11 months to 10 months.

Your reports and your practice coach can help you get very specific about each of these, so that they are all clear, achievable, and ambitious. Then you need a plan.

I was talking to a dentist after a lecture last year, and he was complaining to me that despite all his goal-setting efforts, his practice didn't grow at all and, in fact, production was off 4 percent from the previous year. He was perplexed and questioning the whole goal-setting concept.

I asked him about his process and he told me, "I did what everyone says to do. I made my goals very specific, and I wrote them down."

"That's good," I said. "That's a key step."

"And then, every day I take them out and read them," he continued. "Out loud," he emphasized.

"And?"

"And nothing changed. In fact, things got worse."

"But what did you do to achieve those goals?"

"I told you. I read them every day. Out loud. I even started reading them to my staff in the morning huddle. But nothing changed. The whole process was pointless."

I had to agree with him. It *was* pointless, because he skipped the most important part of goal setting, which is you then have to DO something to achieve those goals. Usually every day. And perhaps even more important: DO SOMETHING DIFFERENT than what you are currently doing.

A GOAL WITHOUT A PLAN IS A WISH.

Just as a dream without a strategy is just a daydream. It is important—critical, I have come to believe—to define your goals and write them down. But then you have to decide what the steps are to achieve them, and commit to doing those steps every day. And if you don't know what the steps are, then you need to get some help to figure it out.

> Clearly define your goals, and then decide what the steps are to achieve them, and commit to doing those steps every day.

Another dentist I encountered two years ago was very down about how the economy in his area had affected his practice, and he asked me what I thought he should do. I gave him a copy of my previous book and suggested he read it and, if it resonated with him, to get his team members to also read it. I ran into him again earlier this year and he proudly told me that his practice was up over 30 percent from two years ago, and he attributed it to what he learned in the book.

But it wasn't because he *read* my book. It was because he decided to *act* on what he had learned in the book. He realized that if he wanted different results, he needed to do something different. You need to be willing to let go of behaviors and systems that may be entrenched.

The answer very often is not to do something harder, or to push your people or yourself harder. If that does yield results, they are often temporary. But most often you need to get outside yourself to figure out what to do differently. So get a practice coach, take a course or three, read books like this one and others that I recommend in the *Resources* section.

Bernie Stoltz, the CEO of Fortune Management, and I often talk about this. Dentists are always looking for the *magic bullet,* that one thing they can do that will make the practice produce a lot more. Ideally for them, it would be something they can buy or tell someone else in the office to do. But the magic bullet, if there is one, isn't magic at all. It comes down to abandoning what is no longer working and putting all your effort into doing the right things. And those things are not unknown. You just don't do them all yet.

Our world is in constant flux. Communication is changing: Try leaving a voicemail and getting a response. Technology is changing: Would you buy a car today without Bluetooth? And consumer behavior is changing: You can deposit checks with your phone, see what a hundred strangers think of a restaurant, and have Amazon deliver your groceries. And you think you can keep doing the same things you've always done? In the face of these changes, that is a recipe for extinction.

So when we set goals, we often plan to put greater effort into doing the same things, instead of trying something different or learning a new approach. But very often a different approach yields exponentially better results. For example, you can spend 10 minutes trying to explain to a patient the decay risk with that ancient amalgam on her second molar with no success. Or you can show her what it looks like using an intraoral or 3-D camera and she'll accept treatment instantly.

You can demand that your appointment administrator do a better job of confirming patients, or you can incentivize her for each new patient she gets in. Or you can hire someone dazzlingly friendly and pay her $10,000 more annually than your competitors do. If she gets one more big restorative case in, she's paid for herself. And if she's trained properly, she'll consistently generate way more than she costs.

Or you can try to place implants using traditional radiography and hope you get the angle and depth right, or you can use GALILEOS and know exactly which implant to use and how to place it, and even create a drill guide so you can practically do it blindfolded and have radically better results in less time. And probably charge less. (Faster, better, more affordable.)

The answers are everywhere, and I'm going to try to give you as many as possible in the coming chapters.

But be assured of this: Goals are pointless without a plan to execute. And as you execute, be sure to sequence your changes. Pick one thing, get it done, make it part of the fabric of your practice, and then go on to the next change. Trying 20 changes all at once is another recipe for failure. So make a plan to reach your goals, decide what you're going to do differently, and then take daily action. Commit to it. Otherwise, this year will be just like last year. Or maybe a little worse.

Work with your team to start making changes, and doing some bold, risky things to make some leaps forward. Stop ignoring what's wrong and attack those things one by one.

BUILDING YOUR
REMARKABLE TEAM

REMARKABLE DENTIST #3

Kirsten L. Romani, DMD
Romani Orthodontics
East Providence and Chepachet, RI
romaniorthodontics.com
facebook.com/romaniorthodontics

Year opened: 2009

REMARKABLE NUMBERS:

Gross profit margin: 48 percent
Annual growth since 2011: 30 percent
New case starts per month: 58
Facebook likes: 3,348

REMARKABLE TECHNOLOGIES:

Dr. Romani uses CBCT, which greatly enhances her ability to diagnose and treat ortho patients. And nothing wows them like 3-D images of themselves.

"The Board." This is what patients call the large touch-screen in the reception area, where anyone can search their town or school and find photos of completed patients from the same place. Her husband Dan designed it, and new patients instantly gravitate to it.

REMARKABLE BEHAVIOR:

Dr. Romani is continually doing contests and is amazingly active in her community, particularly in schools. She has a Tooth Fairy program, where she teaches oral hygiene to 2nd grade classes, set up through the school nurse.

She has a program called *Reading Rocks*, where she has a competition between classes to see which one can read the most total pages, done during National Reading Week in April. She rewards the teacher and students with pizza and t-shirts, and then also donates to the school library.

She's a master team builder. She recently rewarded everyone at a team dinner with new Coach handbags. She bonuses based on new contracts rather than production (she's an ortho, don't forget!): a portion paid monthly, some dropped into a big fund given out before Thanksgiving, and an annual bonus.

She also raises Belted Galloway cows.

WHAT PEOPLE SAY:

"Everyone at the office is so positive and full of energy, and the experience was painless and actually FUN for my daughter. Thank you for seeming to care about her and my family so much. Correcting her smile may be a long journey, but I have great confidence that it will happen— and thank goodness it's an easy process. And thank you for the yummy cup of coffee each time I visit!"

"Dr. Romani and her office staff are outstanding. I was a patient of hers and LOVE my smile, and my husband is currently a patient with Invisalign and is thrilled with his results so far. When my kids are old enough and need braces (which they will), they will be seeing Dr. Romani, without a doubt. She is an outstanding orthodontist and gives back to the community—it doesn't get better than Romani Orthodontics!"

CHAPTER 21

YOUR TEAM IS
YOUR PERSONA

The only way to create a remarkable patient experience is with a remarkable team.

And that means everyone. Quite simply, a dental practice is too small an ecosystem to not have everyone aligned, pulling in the same direction, and supporting one another. Your team is the foundation for all your practice marketing, and they will determine the level of success of your practice to a greater degree than everything else, except perhaps the dentist's case presentation skills.

Dentists often ask me how they can build a great dental team, and my answer always is this: Make your practice a great place to work. Not just how well you pay, but what the practice environment is like. That means creating an exceptional business culture. A culture is defined by how you treat one another, how you treat customers and, more importantly, what you will and you won't do for money. In essence, it starts with the dentist knowing her WHY. Then you need your entire team aligned with that clearly defined purpose.

A culture that attracts great employees has some key elements:

- Everyone is encouraged to learn and grow.
- Everyone is supportive of one another.
- Everyone is honest with one another, including management.
- Everyone holds one another accountable.
- Everyone expresses appreciation often, in many forms.
- Everyone has a sense of accomplishment (the purpose is being fulfilled).
- Everyone contributes to creating a fun, friendly environment.

This doesn't mean people don't work hard. Part of a great culture is having people who really want to accomplish something every day and leave satisfied. Notice one word repeated in each element? Everyone. That means not <u>almost</u> everyone, or just the dentist or the office manager, but all of you.

The right culture attracts top performers and keeps them. The best employees don't only care about money, they care about

The best culture will attract the best team members.

where they work, what they achieve, and who they achieve it with. In the dental field there is an emotional bonus for everyone, which is you're making people's lives better. What a wonderful thing to get to do every day. Capitalize on that advantage. Few jobs can offer that level of satisfaction and purpose.

Another reason why culture is critical is that, unlike most other businesses, there isn't a lot of room for advancement in a dental practice. When you take promotions out of the equation, it makes a strong culture all the more essential to attract and keep the best employees. Of course you may have some team members who do want to go to the next level. Maybe your hygienist has decided to go to dental school. Let her go. Encourage her. Don't fear ambition in your team—feed it. When you encourage people to chase their dreams, to be better and reach further, then everyone perceives that their dreams are important to you, not just your own. That's powerful. That's a practice built on bedrock.

The author Daniel Pink, in his book *Drive*, goes deep into analyzing what truly motivates people at work. The elements are simple and profound: autonomy, growth, and purpose. Wait, what about money? We often think money is the primary motivator. But beyond money, which everyone needs, the team members want a practice that challenges them to learn new technology, where they are surrounded by people who encourage them to be better, with a dentist or office manager who gives them responsibility and inspires them with a higher purpose (that they are in the healing business).

I've said to dental teams many times that there is great nobility in taking care of people in a profession that is underappreciated by the general public. Being a rock star or celebrity, where praise comes at you from every direction is easy, but it eventually rings hollow. Remember my friend Karen's WHY (helping people in spite of themselves)? That is truly admirable. And I think also richly satisfying.

Of course, money is still an important motivator if someone makes less than $40,000 a year. This often slips dentists' minds, as they make much more than that. But at this level of income, gas prices, a speeding ticket, vacation costs, daycare, and education all impact their lives, so I'm not minimizing that. But truly happy people—motivated people—aren't working primarily for the money. But be mindful that money is still an issue, and that incentivizing your team is crucial. I'll talk more about that in Chapter 25.

In my first book, I talked about the principle of hiring for attitude—and it is critical to hire people with a great attitude. But I have learned that to take it to the next level, you need to hire *motivated* people. Not just people who have a positive attitude, but who are driven to do great work every day. And then the goal is to inspire them to provide remarkable service, and to make patients feel comfortable, respected, and cared for.

Inspiring team members requires great leadership. And that requires a commitment to making everyone feel safe, respected, and empowered.

They feel *safe* when the business is running well and profitably, and they don't feel under constant threat of being let go based on the whim of the dentist or the failure of the practice. In short, they don't ever want to feel expendable.

They feel *respected* when they are treated like a peer, like a team member, not an underling. When their opinions are heard, and who they are as a person matters as much as what they contribute to the productivity, they will feel respected.

They feel *empowered* when they are given responsibility and allowed and even encouraged to expand their skills. Micromanaging kills empowerment. Constant critique without solutions or a balance of gratitude kills empowerment.

A remarkable team supports one another. If someone has a personal family issue, the team steps up and covers for them. I recently visited a dental manufacturer's facility with a great work culture. They told me of one employee who had gone blind over the course of his years on the job, and they had rearranged his workspace so that he could still do his job while sightless. But what most impressed me was there was time when he needed surgery, and his leave time exceeded the amount of personal days that he had accrued, and other team members donated their vacation days to him so that he didn't have to go without pay during his recovery.

Now that's a remarkable culture.

And here is the biggest advantage: A great culture attracts the best team members. A remarkable culture is the gravitational pull of great employees. The dental practices I know with a remarkable culture never have trouble attracting or keeping the best employees. Conversely, compromising on your culture is mortgaging your future. Never discount its importance. Simply put, culture attracts quality.

As a side note, nicely designed scrubs with your practice logo on them is a key element of your culture. Think of it like a team uniform. Patients will recognize it, and when employees are on the way to and from work or out to lunch, people will notice and remember the practice name and the nice look.

Lastly, your practice culture is extremely apparent to your patients. And perhaps even more important, you can't build trust with patients with high turnover. Remember, trust is the foundation for case acceptance. High team turnover will diminish the level of trust people feel, because there is no consistency in the practice relationship, no familiarity. And it will have a direct impact on production. Longevity with team members is not only possible, but critical to becoming remarkable.

Trust is diminished by high team turnover.

Define your culture clearly as a team. Write it down and post it. Make your culture part of your interview process. Use websites like DentalPost.net to find new employees, and use their employee profile testing to determine if someone is a good fit for your practice.

Assign the role of Culture Cop to someone on your team. Someone who thinks of events, seeks out inspirational items and actions, and makes sure everyone stays clear on the purpose. Someone who keeps track of the culture and makes it part of the hiring process, review process, and morning huddles and monthly meetings. Someone to monitor where you hit the culture mark and where you're falling short.

When it comes down to building a team, you need to be ruthless. That may sound harsh, but what it really means is that you are protecting the team by protecting the culture, and not hiring anyone who is not a great fit and is not motivated to do a great job. It also means that you are willing to let anyone go who doesn't fit that bill. That's what the next chapter is about.

CHAPTER 22

FIRING IS AN
ACT OF KINDNESS

To build and maintain a great culture, you cannot be afraid to fire people. Tony Hsieh, the CEO of Zappos, is an acquaintance of mine. His company has a phenomenal culture—one of the best I've ever seen. I asked him once what he would have done differently on his way to $2 billion in annual revenue. And he said, "I would have fired people more quickly and hired them more slowly." This from a man who has averaged over $100 million of revenue *growth* every year he's been in business! Every business owner makes this mistake, so don't beat yourself up about it. But resolve to change it. I'm going to give you the thinking that will make it easier to do.

We all know that letting an employee go is one of the most difficult aspects of running a business. It's even more challenging for small businesses, as the team is generally close-knit, and often a friendship develops between the owner or manager and the employee. But the fact remains that to grow any business you need to be constantly examining and improving your team components.

Without an amazing team, you cannot create a large base of loyal patients. No matter how great the dentist's clinical skills, what the patient is going to remember is how friendly, courteous, thoughtful, and compassionate the office team was.

Let's add one more element. Each dentist only has 30-35 hours a week to deliver dentistry. If the dentist exceeds that, it's a physically overwhelming profession, and he will pay the price by shortening his career through exhaustion or disability. So how efficiently you operate during those hours is critical. I can pretty much guarantee you that someone on your team is slowing the whole process down, and everyone knows who that is.

Lastly, a dental practice is a sales organization. If you don't believe or understand that, you haven't read my first book (and you also want to ignore reality). Dentistry is a great service—perhaps more valuable dollar-for-dollar than anything else people spend money on. But as I've pointed out, people have to be talked into it. And that requires that everyone on the team be willing to effectively communicate the value of comprehensive care.

Anyone who's been in business long enough will tell you this, too: None of us has ever regretted firing anyone, only how long we waited to do so. We all do it. We all wait too long. We wait until the disease has infected the entire body. And that's a good metaphor. Very likely one employee is the deep-pocket perio infection in your practice, and you're leaving it untreated. Would you do that with a patient?

My advice is, pull the trigger. There is someone better out there, and the team will take up the slack and respect you for having done it. (Side note: Every day that person stays in your office, the team loses a little more respect for the dentist.)

Why do I say it's an act of kindness to fire someone? Because that person needs to know that they are not performing at the highest level, and therefore will continue to be less and less employable as they grow older. It's actually cruel to wait on your part. Let's say they're 35 now. Are you going to wait until they're 40 to release them into the job market, with their bad work habits more deeply ingrained? It's a wake-up call to get fired. It forces someone to do some self-examination.

Granted, they may not get the message right away. Denial is an easy trap. But letting them continue working for you is reinforcing that they don't have to *do* a great job to *keep* their great job. When I put it that way, it sounds like a pretty ridiculous thing to be doing, doesn't it? Because, if you have a remarkable culture, then they do have a great job. And it's being wasted on them. So it's cruel, or cowardly at least, for the business owner not to step up and let that person know that their performance is insufficient. Cruel to the rest of the team, too. Quite simply, your culture demands it.

A dental practice is too small to have everyone not performing and participating at the same high level.

Here's another important note: They don't have to be a bad employee for you to terminate them. If they don't fit as a team player, if they aren't looking to improve their skills, if they don't choose a great attitude every day and show up motivated to help people, that's enough. Because you need that from everyone. Remember, a dental practice is too small to have anyone not performing and participating at the same high level.

The steps are simple: When you have an employee not performing, spell out in detail exactly what your expectations are from them for improvement, with a timeline, and do it in writing. And let them know that if they do not meet or exceed those expectations, after that time period they will no longer be employed. (I recommend 30 days maximum.) I also believe in giving severance, along with a detailed termination agreement. I recommend using a service like HR for Health to button up all these sorts of things in your practice. There is a proper and legal way to do this to protect yourself.

I know you hate doing it. I do too. But I've had a number of employees over the years come back and thank me for giving them that message and helping them get on track, by either finding a job that suits them, fixing their attitude, or learning to be a better employee. So find that infection and treat it now. You'll feel better in the morning.

CHAPTER 23

GRATITUDE
IS JOB ONE

Unexpressed gratitude is like dying with a lot of money in the bank. In fact, it's even worse, because you can't leave it as part of your estate. It's a terrible waste. Your team needs to know you appreciate them, in some way, every day. It shouldn't just be praise, which of course is essential, but I also recommend a surprise gift or a sudden field trip or unexpected reward. Appreciation and encouragement elevates your team to its highest level. And many business owners neglect this—or worse—don't think it's necessary. Your team members aren't just employees, they're human beings. They don't show up just to make money. Creating an environment of thankfulness becomes the glue that holds a remarkable practice together.

Neglecting it ignores human nature and replaces it with ideas like, "People should be grateful to have jobs," or some other "should" that is irrelevant because that's not how people respond or think. A clear example of how profound an effect gratefulness has both on your success and the well-being of your team was demonstrated by research done by Robert Emmons and Michael McCollough.[12] They did a study with three groups of people and gave each a different assignment.

1. The first group was told to write daily about anything they wanted.
2. The second group was told to list bad or negative experiences.
3. The third group was told to write daily all the things that they were grateful for.

The net result was that the last group exhibited higher levels of enthusiasm, optimism, determination, and alertness—plus they were more energetic, made more progress in achieving their personal goals, and even exercised more regularly. And the second group, who focused on the negative, had significantly worse results than both other groups.

Only 13 percent of Americans love their jobs.[13] Why create a place that people don't like going to, when it's not necessary and so simple to solve?

This approach to gratitude has to become systematic, ingrained into your behavior as the dentist and as a team member, and integrated into the fabric of your practice as part of your day. Gratitude toward your coworkers, toward your patients, and toward the businesses and individuals that support your success—from coaches and consultants, to your distributor rep, to your equipment support people, and your lab—yields dividends that may not be precisely measurable, but the results will be profound.

1-800-DENTIST has a customer service department that handles all the issues and concerns of our clients. It's a tough job, because people often don't know how to express themselves sanely and calmly when things didn't go the way they expected, so my team can get a lot of heat. No company delivers a perfect product, and neither do we. We just try to make it right when we don't and try to learn from our mistakes. But our customer service team deals with a hefty amount of negativity throughout the day, and very seldom do they experience appreciation from the callers they are helping.

So it falls on their manager and the rest of us in the company to make sure we express it, and let them know how much we appreciate the role they perform as the pressure release valve, so that we can all keep doing what we do. This comes in many forms, but we've found it's almost impossible to do too much of it.

We also try to balance their experiences with the positive feedback that we get from patients, members, and dentists we encounter at dental conventions and office visits.

Your dental team will deal with negativity from patients in various forms, from complaints about cost and insurance, to discomfort and confusion about how significant their dental problems are. And people are often not polite. Nothing heals a rough encounter like expressing appreciation to that person who took the bullet for the team. Every team member needs to be comfortable expressing appreciation and gratitude, especially the dentist. It only takes a minute or two out of a day. Once you do it—and see the visible reactions—you'll become addicted to doing it.

And if someone in your office doesn't want to do it, you have to question what they are doing on your team.

Some examples of what to say:

> "You really handled that patient's anxiety well. I couldn't have done it better myself."

> "These donuts are because you are all amazing and make my life easy, so I wanted to make your mouths happy."

> "Time for a team selfie!"

> "I look forward to being here every day, because I know you're all going to be here making it a great day."

> "I know it's your son's birthday, so here's $20 to get him something nice, but don't tell him it was from me."

> "Clear the schedule for next Wednesday afternoon. We're going bowling."

And you can also plan all sorts of fun events—not just lunches together—like:

- Shoe shopping
- Disneyland or Six Flags
- Pool hall day
- Bowling
- Karaoke night

Then there are dental meetings that are fun and team building, like the Madow Brothers' The Best Seminar Ever and the annual meeting of the American Association of Dental Office Managers, or SIRO World, Sirona's new annual digital dentistry meeting. Make sure you go to at least one big one and a few smaller ones each year. I know it's easy to get CE online now, but I think the value of learning together in a live environment goes beyond just the information being conveyed. The social element and group participation add a deeper dimension to the experience, and make the learning last longer while bonding the team closer.

And don't forget the impact of charity events that the whole team participates in. Whether you are doing a free day of dentistry in your community, going off together to a foreign country to donate your skills for a week, or any other community event, few things will bond a team more closely than helping those in need.

Lastly, don't discount the power of constructive criticism. Part of having a great culture is having team members who want to be getting better at what they do, but often they don't know what that is, so they need to be guided. The caveat is that if you don't pair that with an environment of gratitude, they don't improve because they don't think it will be noticed. So notice when they get better. Vocalize what they can do to improve and what they've achieved. Celebrate victories and achievements as a team.

CHAPTER 24

THE FRONT DESK
DILEMMA

The night before a lecture in San Antonio, I was having dinner with my hosts and their spouses, and one of the wives, whose career was in marketing, asked me, "In your 30 years of doing this, what's the one biggest thing you've observed that holds dental practices back from succeeding?"

My answer was instantaneous. "The front desk," I said. "No other industry could survive the waste that occurs there in the average practice."

"How bad is it?" she probed.

"It is the least trained, worst paid, most mismanaged position in the entire practice."

"Really? What do you think that costs the average practice?"

"Between $100 and $200 thousand in production, every year," was my response. She was aghast.

So how do you solve this? It's simple economics. Put a well-trained, well-paid person in the position, and they will pay for themselves two or three times over. And on top of that, all your patients will have a better experience when calling the practice or walking in. Group practices are all learning that they simply can't multitask this position. It's too important. So learn what the groups already have, or they will out-do you.

> **Put a well-trained, well-paid person at the front desk, and they will pay for themselves two or three times over.**

I know that turnover is high at the front desk, but it's very often because of how most dentists regard the position. We have some operators at 1-800-DENTIST who've been there for 10 or 15 years, still doing an amazing job. Like any important position in a business—and the front desk is the aorta of your practice—underpaying is a poor strategy.

Why do I call it underpaying? Market rate for the position may be around $28,000-$30,000, but market rate is failing. Let's do the math. Let's say a good new patient case produces $4,000. If you miss one good case a month, that's 12 in a year. That's $48,000 in missed revenue. And it could happen because the patient went to voicemail, or the front desk administrator was busy and indifferent on the phone, or didn't answer insurance questions well—the list is endless. So with a margin on new cases of 80 percent (remember my point about escaping gravity in Chapter 7), you've missed out on $38,400 of *profit*. This to me demonstrates how crucial this position is to your practice and how "market rate" is obviously undervaluing the position.

The solution is simple. Pay over market. Get two people if the calls are going to voicemail. Incentivize them for getting new patients to show up, regardless of how much the patient ends up spending. And train them well.

So how do you get them properly trained? In the *Resources* section I list a few companies that do this very well. The key is to record the phone conversations and have the team members listen with you, and coach them on what they did right, and where they might have gone off course. Many times they will identify their own mistakes and say, "Wow, I talked to the patient for 10 minutes and never asked them if they wanted an appointment," or "I can tell I'm not smiling on that call."

There is also rule of thumb on coaching from a recording, which is that the ratio of praise to critique should be 2:1, meaning twice as many positive comments as negative. Otherwise, the person is overwhelmed with the amount of criticism and doesn't have a balance of positive reinforcement.

I also recommend fixing your front desk before investing in any advertising, because the waste will make it so you can't discern what promotions might actually be working.

CHAPTER 25

REWARDING
YOUR TEAM

If you've read my first book, you know that I believe that you should incentivize your team based on hitting predetermined goals. I also strongly recommend bonusing the whole team proportional to their income, not singling out individuals and giving different ranges of bonuses to each based on their roles.

Now I've discovered a new twist that gets the team really focused: weekly bonuses. Instead of doing it monthly, which I previously suggested, I've found practices getting great results by doing their incentives based on hitting the goal for the week. This keeps the team's eyes on the prize. A month often seems a little far off, and as you get close to the end of the month it can be challenging to rally enough to recover from lagging production. But with weekly goals, it makes them think about the production on a daily basis.

Try it for a few months. I've heard of a few brilliant successes with it, but I'd love to hear more practices' results.

A little side note on embezzlement—which, by the way, will happen to one out of four dentists in the course of his or her career. I sincerely believe that underpaying your team and not incentivizing them will hurt your long-term growth, while deceptively increasing your short-term wealth. But one of the other results is it generates resentment on the team.

Think about it. The dentist is making more and more money, the team knows it is producing more, yet they get the same pay they always did. It's dispiriting and invites some less ethical people to try to balance the scales. Shockingly, embezzlement is almost always done by the person the dentist suspects least. But it is perhaps the most disturbing thing that will happen in a dentist's career.

Embezzlement results from a combination of envy, resentment, contempt, and petty thievery that starts small and then escalates. And it happens when the dentist does one specific thing and fails to do another.

The first cause is when the dentist not only doesn't reward the team, but also spends visibly on his lifestyle, basically rubbing it in his employees' faces. This communicates, "I deserve this, and you don't. I did it all by myself." No bonus, but the wife has a new Mercedes. No team incentive, but the dentist and her family fly first class to Paris for two weeks.

The second cause is relinquishing control of the finances. You're essentially leading others into temptation. Remember when I said your practice is too small not to sign your own checks? That's key. Also, not knowing how to read your financial statements and practice reports, or not looking at credit card statements. Embezzlement usually starts with the perpetrator finding out that you don't notice that they money is missing. So the amount increases the next time they need it. And before you know it, it's tens of thousands, and sometimes hundreds. And I hope you realize that even if you catch the person, the stolen money is long gone.

If you're the dentist, do what it takes to prevent this from happening. If you're a team member and suspect something, alert the dentist, because this is going to severely damage the practice emotionally and financially—perhaps permanently—if it continues.

REMARKABLE INCENTIVES

A remarkable team deserves remarkable rewards. One of the first things I recommend is splitting your team bonuses between cash and contributions to their retirement plan, which you can easily set up. (See the system offered in Tony Robbins' money book in the *Resources* section.)

A remarkable team deserves remarkable rewards.

Help your team build a spirit of saving for the future. One of the great tortures most people inflict on themselves is living right at the edge of their means. If you create a retirement plan where employees compete with one another to see who can save the most, suddenly you have people who don't have to turn to you in a crisis because their car broke down or they had some medical need in the family, and they will eventually reach a point where their savings really start to look like something. You will build a team that has financial peace of mind.

I remember this story about the cast of *Friends*—one of the most successful sitcoms of all time—where the actors were earning $1 million per episode by the end. Instead of blowing their money on cars and clubs and extensive entourages, they competed with each other to see who could buy the most investment real estate. This gave them all genuine security in an industry where there is almost none. Unlike many actors who finally get on a show and start spending excessively, they brought sanity to their lives.

Beyond just production bonuses and incentives, you can get really creative with rewards for your team. Team adventures and events, big and small, also bind you together, as I mentioned earlier. They don't have to be expensive, either. Here are some ideas, but it should be the team that comes up with them. Some suggestions:

- A miniature golf excursion with valuable prizes
- A cruise for the team and their spouses
- A group barbecue
- New team photos every year, sometimes in costume, sometimes at events
- Working at a charity event that the team members choose

And here are some interesting alternative cash bonuses:

- $100 for best patient story of the month (video it, of course)
- $50 for the most new patients brought in by handing out business cards
- $1 for every email address
- $1,000 for bringing in the patient who became the biggest case of the year

For some of the more extravagant events, I know dentists who use this technique: To pay for the team excursion, everyone agrees to work an extra day that month, and all the production income is dedicated to the cause. It may even take several months to save the money, but if the prize is worth it, everyone gets excited about pitching in.

Take the whole team to marketing and clinical training events at least twice a year. And wrap a little playtime around it. You will always learn something new or be reminded of something that you should be doing that you stopped, but you will also build team spirit and unity in a way that you can't in the office alone.

Remember that in a dental practice there is very little opportunity to move up or radically increase your income, unlike larger corporations. And the days can blend together. Give your team something to look forward to and give them a chance to earn it.

And one last profound observation, from author Seth Godin: You don't build an extraordinary team by offering them an ordinary job.

SECTION FIVE:

REMARKABLE ACTIONS

REMARKABLE DENTIST #4

Nhi T. Pham, DDS
Mukilteo Dental Center
Mukilteo, WA
mukilteodentalcenter.com
facebook.com/mukilteodental

Year opened: 2003

REMARKABLE NUMBERS:

New patients per month: 75 or so. All from word-of-mouth.
Annual revenue: Not sure. But her husband tells her she's
   had 10x growth since she opened. Also, with each preg-
   nancy, her production went up.
Total patients: 4,000+
Associates: 1

REMARKABLE TECHNOLOGIES:

CEREC, soft tissue lasers, digital radiography, intraoral
cameras

REMARKABLE BEHAVIOR:

Dr. Pham has built a practice founded in gratitude and charity. She spent the first four years of her career in the National Service Corp., and that experience set the tone for everything in her practice. She sees herself and all her team as servant leaders.

She embraces technology early, but believes in patient relationships above all. She believes if she takes care of the team, they will take care of the patients. She is not big on knowing the numbers.

She calls the team her "Phamily," and they celebrate everything, and make a continuous effort to express gratitude and appreciation to their patients.

She does volunteer dentistry one day a week.

She teaches at the University of Washington dental school one day a week, instilling values and expounding on how building a relationship with the patient makes it easier to treat them.

Each year the practice celebrates the Spirit of Aloha, where the entire office goes into Hawaii mode, with clothing, decorations, and attitude. And she pairs it with a food drive.

Freedom Day is another charitable event, where she offers free dentistry to veterans and their families. Volunteers from the community— both dentists and non-dentists— participate, bringing food and joining the party and honoring the service of the veterans.

She doesn't have her own desk or private office inside the practice.

Dr. Pham learned to be more public with her charitable behavior so that other people would feel inspired to do the same.

REMARKABLE QUOTES:

"Everyone wants to go to a party—no one wants to go to a funeral."

"My practice is really not about dentistry, but rather a foundation for a bigger vision, a platform that offers patients and team members personal fulfillment, creates jobs that support families and provides for community outreach projects, encouraging everyone to be a global citizen."

WHAT PEOPLE SAY:

"I'm not a fan of going to the dentist, but let's be honest, who is? Yet every time I come in here—even after I had a wisdom tooth pulled—I leave in a good mood. The staff is absolutely wonderful and the dentists are such sweethearts. I wouldn't even consider going anywhere else."

"From the moment you walk in and talk to the girls at the front desk, to the end of your visit, it's as great an experience as going to the dentist can be. Dr. Pham is wonderful and personable, and she really cares about your teeth and your comfort. I have moved to Renton and I still drive to Mukilteo for my dental cleaning and work—I refuse to go anywhere else!"

"I am a new patient here and I love it. I usually dread going to the dentist because my teeth are incredibly sensitive. I couldn't believe how easy all of my appointments have been. Dr. Pham and her staff are also good at explaining what's happening, why it's happening, and your options. They are so polite and helpful. (Plus there is a TV at every chair.) Best dentist and hygienists I've ever had."

CHAPTER 26

NOBODY SHOULD
LEAVE WITHOUT...

Here are some rules, both old and new, about practice and team behavior:

- Nobody should ever leave your office without paying in full. (Why bill them? So you can guarantee that 10 percent of it won't be collected?)
- Nobody should leave without having "checked in" on Facebook.
- Nobody should leave without updating their cell phone number and email address and contact preferences.
- Nobody should leave without their next appointment scheduled. (They all have smart phones with calendars.)
- Nobody should leave without being asked to recommend the practice to their friends.
- Nobody should leave your practice because their insurance changed without being told that they are always welcome to come back if they miss the care you've provided, and that they can always call you with questions

when someone else recommends treatment. (This lets them know you care about *them*—not money—and that they don't have to be embarrassed about leaving you because they were trying to save money. Often, they will miss your care and go out of network to come back.)

- Nobody should leave without a goody bag of some kind, ideally one with items appropriate for their treatment (like toothpaste, a toothbrush, travel floss, fluoride treatment, ibuprofen, and home-care instructions).
- Nobody should ever leave without a fond farewell *and* an expressed sentiment about their next visit. (See the following chapter.)

Most of you do some of these, most of the time. Imagine if you did it with everyone, all the time. You'd collect 100 percent of your fees, grow your practice with new patients, save time at the front desk, and all your patients would feel valued and appreciated. You'd be pretty darn remarkable. Why? Because most of your competitors aren't doing these things consistently—or at all. They make it easy for you to stand out.

CHAPTER 27

APPLE RETAIL
TRAINING

Apple stores have been open for over 10 years now, and they average five times the revenue per square foot of the next highest retail store. They train their retail employees in a very specific way. This is all part of their brand experience, which I'm sure I don't have to explain is wildly successful around the world.

This is what the retail team is taught:

Approach the customer with a warm, personalized greeting
Probe politely to understand all the customer's needs
Present a solution for the customer to take home that day
Listen for and resolve any issues or concerns
End with a fond farewell and an invitation to return

Why wouldn't you want to incorporate every one of these behaviors into your practice? Especially since you know how effective they are. Just replace the word "customer" with patient. Let's break it down.

A warm, personalized greeting. Who doesn't want that? More often than not, you know the patient's name, and if you don't, you should find out quickly and make introductions to other team members. Warm *and* personalized. To everyone. Chisel it in stone.

Probing politely to understand the patient's needs. This in part is the hygienist's role, but also the dentist's. All good case presentation starts with knowing what the patient's problem is and what level of priority it is for them. "Probe" means something more than just "ask." You're teasing it out of them, knowing that there are layers of trust that still have to be built.

Present a solution that can be completed that day. Not always possible, but you want to do as much as you can. If you have CEREC, that expands the possibility considerably. But certainly get them out of pain, reduce the infection if there is any, and lay out the next steps.

Listen. Every team member should be tuned in to what the patient might have as concerns or personal issues. And remarkable case presentation requires keen listening skills. These are developed over time, and as the dentist or treatment coordinator you should be refining your skills and reminding yourself of the fundamentals on an ongoing basis.

Ending with a fond farewell is absolutely essential. I would modify Apple's 'invitation to return" to simply mentioning when the patient will be in next, such as, "See you in two weeks," or "We look forward to seeing you again in June," (which of course requires the person in reception to know when they will return).

This refinement in communication is so important that the next three chapters are devoted to it entirely.

CHAPTER 28

THE RIGHT
WORDS

Having a great team is essential, but for that team to perform at its peak, everyone has to be great a communicator. In my first book, I cover some key recommendations on the right words to use in various situations. But nothing will make this easier than knowing your WHY. When you know that your purpose is helping people get healthy in spite of themselves, for example, it's much easier to come up with the right communication approach.

Let's say a patient asks, "Why don't you take my dental insurance?" If your WHY is to make a lot of money, you're likely to explain that the plan doesn't pay enough for you to treat the patient. But if your WHY is helping people in spite of themselves, you're much more likely to say, "We want to offer you the best care possible, using the best techniques and technologies, while still making it as affordable as possible. Unfortunately, some plans pay so little that it's not possible for us to maintain our standard of care. And we really want what's best for you and your smile."

Note that most often you will have to explain the difference between health care and dental coverage. I recommend making it clear with patients who have dental plans exactly what the difference is by saying something like, "Although it's easy to get it confused, dental coverage isn't like your health insurance, where the doctor charges or hospital charges a very high amount if you don't have coverage and accepts a much lower payment if you do. That's not dental coverage. Dental coverage is a discount on basic care and has almost nothing to do with what is being diagnosed as necessary. With health care, the more extreme your need, the more coverage you have. Dental coverage actually limits how much overall treatment it will pay for each year, regardless of your need. They are not concerned with what is required to preserve your teeth and keep them healthy as long as possible, but only with their own guidelines and limits. It's our job—our professional responsibility, in fact—to tell you what you actually need and what treatment would help you stay your healthiest."

It's a rather lengthy explanation, but an important one to offer. Do you see how it leads the patient away from the misconception that their dental plan knows how much treatment they need and shifts their thinking to getting healthy?

Basic rule of effective communication: Always talk in terms of the benefit to the patient.

One of the basic rules of effective communication is to always talk in terms of the benefit to the patients—which then means avoiding clinical terminology. So don't say radiography, say X-rays. Not CAD/CAM, but rather, our in-house laboratory that makes it possible for us to finish your treatment in a single visit. And consistency is important. Whether explaining your technology or any other aspect of your practice and treatment, every team member needs to be singing from the same choir book.

Often the right words come down to asking the right questions, such as:

- "How important is your oral health?"
- "Are you comfortable?"
- "Do you have any concerns about the treatment?"
- "Do you need some way to signal me if you need a break?"

This last one is more important than you may think. During a longer procedure, verbalizing that you understand what they're going through will reduce their anxiety and take away some of the stress associated with the loss of control the patient feels. I call it giving the patient a comfort break—stopping halfway through the procedure to let them relax for a minute or two.

Don't be afraid to inject a little personality into your chairside conversations. Done properly, it will put people at ease, especially with something they might already be uncomfortable about. A good example would be the hygienist doing her oral cancer exam. She could say, "Now I'm going to check for oral cancer. Don't freak out; we always do it. It's for your own good to catch it early. Plus, it's our job." Saying things like this show that you are tuned in to what they are experiencing and feeling, rather than just what you are trying to accomplish. It can be very powerful.

Some dentists are afraid to talk about money. That communicates—erroneously—that they don't truly believe in the value of what they offer. Now, you may believe in your dentistry and work very hard at being a highly skilled clinician, but when you are afraid to talk about money, the patient gets the impression that you don't believe it's worth it. That is why you have to get comfortable—in fact, confident—when it comes to talking about the cost of the treatment plan. Because unquestionably it *is* a good investment, and the patient is looking to you for your professional recommendation, even if they don't particularly like it. Remember, you're helping people in spite of themselves.

A very effective method of persuasion and helping patients understand is the use of analogies. For example, when a patient wants to do only the treatment that their insurance covers, ask them, "Would you do that with your car, only repair what is covered under warranty? What if you get a flat? Or you need new brakes? You still have to fix it, even if it you have to pay for it yourself. Isn't your own body as important as your car?"

What job does that patient do for a living? Are they an attorney? A farmer? A schoolteacher? Think in terms of analogies that they will understand and that relate to their field. Humans respond to information that has a context for them.

Also, don't assume your patients know everything you offer, or that they remember just because you told them once. Basic marketing means telling people over and over what you do and why it benefits them. The reason is for the most part, they're not listening or storing the information, because it's not relevant at the moment, or they dismiss it because they can't afford it right then, regardless of how valuable or even necessary it might be.

For example, I'm still shocked at how many seniors have never heard of dental implants, despite being denture wearers. Or they have an outdated understanding of the procedure—that it takes six months and involves a lot of surgery and discomfort. A friend of mine recently told me of a new patient who had been wearing dentures for seven years, and when he mentioned implants to her, she was surprised the alternative existed. She had ample means to pay and started the treatment immediately. My friend subsequently has done implants for every woman in his patient's bridge club. (No pun intended.)

Therein lies another challenge with your patients: They have misconceptions about treatment options based on information they gathered 10 or even 20 years ago. What a great opportunity to be remarkable. The right words at the right time make all the difference.

CHAPTER 29

STOP SELLING
DENTISTRY
RATIONALLY

I know that the urge to sell, to persuade people with rational thought, is compelling. And I realize that dentists are scientists and very methodical in their daily procedures, which follow a rational progression to completion. But a purely rational approach seldom works with dental patients.

A purely rational approach seldom works with dental patients.

The difference between a dentist and most medical professionals is that when people see a physician, they have a medical condition that they are likely already aware of, and they also trust implicitly what the physician tells them has to be done—particularly if it's surgery. Conversely, they see most of what you tell them as optional, like buying a first-class seat instead of coach. Remember that statistic from earlier, that 31 percent of consumers believe dentists are trying to sell them unnecessary treatment. In part this is because their teeth have been "fine" up to this point, and also because they don't believe they're going to die from dental neglect. You are not holding their life in your hands, but they believe—rightly or wrongly— that the physician is.

Do you think heart surgeons have a 30 percent acceptance rate when they recommend a bypass to a patient? Not likely. So you need a higher level of trust and a more effective level of persuasion in order to have your treatment plan accepted.

We all like to believe that we behave rationally. And that other people do too. But we all do things on a regular basis that betray this belief. We text and drive, we buy things we can't afford, we eat bad food on a regular basis, and we ignore obvious truths and do what we feel like doing. Most of the time we are in reflex drive, and this autopilot is programmed with learned behavior—much of it from our childhood—that is skewed sometimes radically away from rational behavior.

A typical example: A friend of mine runs a charity. When she puts on a big fundraiser, with excellent food and drink, and celebrity guests, and everyone dressed to the nines, she will raise a staggering amount of money for the cause. And she is given a commission—a bonus—based on how successful the event is. Now, wouldn't it make more sense to have a much less expensive event, with a cash bar, in a low-cost venue? And yet anytime she attempts such an event, she raises a fraction of the money she would using the elaborate gala approach. The reason is simple: We are subtly but powerfully motivated by emotional drivers, not rational ones.

We are not practical. Why would a man buy a car that does 200 miles an hour when the speed limit is at most 70? Or how could a Hermès Birkin® handbag be worth $20,000 to anyone? What would you need to be carrying in it to justify that expense? But for the wealthy person buying it, it serves a higher purpose, which is to say, "You can't afford this. I can." That is not rational. Rational would be understanding that a handbag is to carry things. The entire fashion industry is driven by irrationality. Why would a woman pay $1,000 for a dress that she will only wear one time? Why would a teenager wear his jeans so low that he has to walk bowlegged to keep them up?

Don't think for one minute that we behave rationally. Our autopilot is preprogrammed with mostly irrational lines of code.

As I said, I understand that as scientists you feel compelled to explain everything to your patients, thinking that's what will convince them to spend their money wisely on their health. But accept the realities of human nature. They can't wait to leave your office without accepting treatment and go spend the money on something stupid. It's up to you to persuade them otherwise, with cues from your practice environment and the words that hit emotional buttons, not just rational ones.

CHAPTER 30

THE FINE ART OF
SHUTTING UP

This skill I'm going to discuss here is primarily for the dentists and treatment coordinators. It's a principle of persuasive communication (and as any remarkable dentist knows, successful dentistry involves effective communication in order to facilitate treatment acceptance). Human nature is what it is, and human behavior—though often irrational—is often quite predictable.

Hence "the fine art of shutting up." Let me show you how this is applied. Think about this typical situation in a dental office: You have presented the treatment plan to the patient and explained the cost, and now you ask, "What do you think?" Then you wait. Silently. Most dentists (and many salespeople, too) can't bear more than a few seconds of silence before jumping in with another thought. Very often it's something like, "If this seems like too much, you don't have to do it right now." Or, "Maybe this is more than you can afford. We have other options." Now the patient is off the hook—and also thinks that perhaps you were overselling them. And you've done that patient a disservice, because most likely the treatment you recommended would be one of the best investments they will make in their life.

Truly great salespeople can do this and wait 10 minutes without uttering a word. Why? **Because you don't know what the person is going to say!** One of the problems with having a good amount of experience is that we believe we can figure out how people are going to respond ahead of time. But there is no upside in making that guess. Let them respond, so you can determine what their real objection might be, or if they even have one. Don't fill in the blank yourself.

To give you an example from my own life, I was having a conversation with a meeting planner who was trying to book me as a speaker. It was an event at which I really wanted to present, as I knew it would be fun and have a great audience. The planner asked me what my honorarium was and I told him my full fee. But then I *almost* said, "But for this event I'd be willing to do it for half that." Luckily, at the last second I remembered the rule and I shut up. I waited. And you know what he said? "That's fine." I would have shorted myself half my fee if I hadn't clammed up.

I get that this is difficult. In fact, this is perhaps the hardest skill to develop in business and in sales. And the longer you're waiting, the harder it is to stay silent. I know, I've been in that situation often. And in fact, most of the time the other person is waiting for *you* to speak and hopefully give them another option. Don't. Just shut up and find out what they really are thinking.

If you've made your treatments faster, better, and more afford-able, that's all the more reason that the patient should be will-ing to begin as soon as possible. If not, something else needs to be explained or clarified. Find out what that actually is. Often, once they tell you their concern, you can simply say, "So if it weren't for that, you would begin the treatment?" And once again, wait. If they say yes, address the expressed concern. If they say no, continue to probe to find out what the real concern is.

For example, if they say, "That seems like a lot of money," then your response would be, "So if cost were not a factor, you would start this treatment today?" Then shut up. If they say yes, then you say, "Let me explain what financial options we have." If they say no, then you know that you haven't gotten to the real objection yet. Most likely they don't appreciate the value or the importance or the urgency of the treatment. But you won't know unless you let them speak first.

Another big bonus to shutting up is that you get to listen in-stead of thinking about what you're going to say next. Once you've decided not to speak, you don't have to think about your response, because you aren't going to say anything until the other person does. It's very powerful, because listening without anticipation is a challenge for most people.

I'll repeat that key thought: *It's not about planning what you will say next.* Your full attention is on the other person. Because lis-tening closely—attentively—will give you the real insight that you need once they finally do speak. You will find out if they don't understand the treatment, the cost, or the importance of it, or if they just want to start. And not only will this inform your response to this patient, it will also give you feedback on where you might be weak in your case presentation, so you can be more effective the next time.

This is not a trick. This is effective communication. And this applies to many different communications that occur in a practice. It's so easy to jump in with our own thoughts after a question or to fill in the silence with more of our own words. But it's not effective.

It's so easy to jump in with our own thoughts after asking a question. But it's not effective.

When you meet a new patient and you sit them down and ask, "How do you feel about your smile?" wait, and see what they say. They could be perfectly happy with their mangled grille, or they could be deeply embarrassed about a minor malocclusion. Don't offer your opinion until you hear theirs. Then tailor your response accordingly.

Practice the fine art of shutting up, and I promise it will yield surprising dividends.

CHAPTER 31

ANSWERING
THE DREADED
MONEY QUESTION

M ore new patients are calling to ask about fees than ever
before. As I mentioned earlier, this is in part because of
the recession and the number of people who have moved down
on the socioeconomic scale. But it's also because people can
now find the price of almost anything using their cell phone.

The other reason is they don't know what else to ask when they
call a dental practice, so they ask about cost. Since we know
the average person does not know how to evaluate a dental
practice with regard to clinical skills, they at least want to find
out what they're going to be paying.

So how do you answer? Most consultants will say that you
should never quote fees over the phone. Most front desk team
members have either never heard this rule or don't follow it.
Some even offer fees without being asked.

I try to discourage receptionists from getting into money over the phone. But it really depends on what type of office you operate. I will break them down into three types:

1. The high-end, high-tech practice (usually a high percent fee-for-service)
2. The PPO practice with mid-range fees
3. The HMO/State Aid/credit dentist practice

HOW TO RESPOND WHEN YOU ARE A HIGH-END PRACTICE:

"We don't normally quote fees over the phone. Our dentist likes to do an evaluation of the patient and then recommend the best treatment. We don't accept most insurance because we want to offer the highest standard of care possible, and most dental coverage is insufficient for that level of treatment. We do have a wonderful office, and patients love us—and we are happy to do an evaluation at no charge to you, so you can see the dentist and the practice and decide for yourself. And we also have several financing options. Would you like to come in tomorrow?" (Your state may have different rules regarding free evaluations.)

HOW TO RESPOND AS A PPO PRACTICE:

"Our fees are very reasonable for our area, and we do accept insurance plans and have financing options. But we really think you'd like our office, so we recommend coming in to get a free evaluation. We won't charge you for anything without your approval, so you'll always understand the cost ahead of time, because we know that's important. Can you come in this afternoon?"

If they keep pressing for a dollar amount, saying things like, "I just need to know how much a crown is at your office," then respond with this:

"It sounds like you might be looking for the least expensive dentist. That isn't us. But we recommend coming in to see the type of practice we are and the level of care that we offer, so when you do find the lowest cost dentist you have something to compare it to. And, of course, we won't charge you for the evaluation."

If they insist on the actual dollar amount, I would give them a range, explaining that it's impossible to do an accurate diagnosis over the phone.

HOW TO RESPOND WHEN YOU ARE AN HMO/STATE AID PRACTICE:

"Our fees are the lowest in the area, and we accept HMO plans (or State Aid), and have excellent financing options for whatever is not covered by this insurance. We don't offer free dentistry, however, so there has to be some financial arrangement made before treatment begins. Can you come in this afternoon?"

Notice that I addressed the issue of "free dental work" right up front. It's critical to be clear about that, as very often their expectation is that you are like a hospital emergency room and the county or state pays for everything. (As a side note, in 2014, ER visits for dentistry in the U.S. cost more than $1 billion. And it usually cost 10 times more at the ER than it would in your office, and seldom is treatment completed.[14])

If they are asking about something specific like an extraction, I would then tell them the cost of treatment. Your business model is to be the least expensive. They're price shopping, so if they want to pay even less than you charge, you probably don't want them as a patient.

THE THINKING BEHIND THIS

The cost of dentistry is definitely a factor for three-quarters of Americans, so don't be dismissive of this concern. But don't just throw a number back at them. Very often they are really trying to find out if they will be treated fairly and don't know what else to ask. When you say, "Our fees are reasonable for the area," this gives them a frame of reference.

You have two goals in every call:

1. Shift their focus off the cost of an individual procedure
2. Get them into the practice

(With the low-cost practice, your third goal is to be extremely clear that your treatments are not free beyond what's covered in their HMO plan.)

This is important to remember: No matter what you do or say, YOU WILL NOT GET EVERYONE IN! But you will improve your chances of starting the relationship right by making it about the care you offer, not the price you charge.

Most of this language I've learned from the masters of communication, Linda Miles and Dr. Paul Homoly, but there are many more fine teachers out there. Getting good at effective communication with regard to cost is essential, so get expert training where you need it.

CHAPTER 32

PATIENTS ARE LIKE PETS: TRAIN THEM

My dog begs. It's no surprise—I trained her to do it. It was easy. I didn't even intend to. She also sleeps on the couch. That was even easier to train her to do. I just allowed her to do it and I was done!

We often complain about how patients behave when, in reality, we taught them it's okay to behave that way.

Very often we complain about how patients behave when, in reality, we taught them or at least allowed them to behave that way. They cancel appointments at the last minute, they pay us when and if they feel like it, they make us contact them three times to confirm an appointment, they complain when their insurance doesn't pay for everything, they get two years behind in their cleanings, they wear temporaries for six months. You know what I'm talking about.

Of course, it takes time and effort to train your dog to respect your dinner, your carpet, and your couch. But it's usually worth it. Same thing with patients. My personal opinion is that there should be no such thing as accounts payable in a dental practice. Get paid for what you do when you do it. (I know, it sounds crazy!) For decades, we have trained patients that we will bill them later.

What that has averaged out to be for most practices is 10 percent uncollectible. But I know many practices that are now getting the fee handled *before starting the procedure.* It can be done, and you end up getting 100 percent of your money. You may not be ready for this, but in any case patients should never leave the office with an outstanding balance that is not financed or reimbursed by their dental plan.

As a side note, I've been told by those in the know in the finance world that getting fee approval chairside has become a no-no. Some states are apparently considering it coercion. So to be on the safe side, have a separate presentation room where all this is discussed with the patient. Much as I love the idea of them just signing off on the additional treatment while they're sitting in the operatory, I wouldn't risk it.

This principle of retraining also applies to missed appointments or last-minute cancellations. Hey, we all lead busy lives, and sometimes something comes up, and we all deserve a pass now and then. But you know who your abusers are, and they are putting holes in your schedule that you can't fill. Now, I don't believe in charging for missed appointments. That just loses the money and the patient.

But with your patients who take a casual view of your schedule, after the second time it happens I would tell them that you can no longer hold appointments for them unless they prepay. You're happy to call them if you have a last-minute opening (from some other "casual" patient), but tell them that without enough notice, they are preventing you from taking care of other patients who need treatment and *can* show up, and show up on time. By the way, don't throw the words "practice policy" around. That is not persuasive. Make it about not being able to treat other patients.

I know that it's hard to train existing patients who already have the wrong behavior. So why not at least start with your new patients? Train them the right way from the first visit. Within a year or two, you will have had a significant impact on the activity in your office, and most likely on your productivity as well. You've only got so many hours a week to treat patients, and every gap in the schedule is a treatment you can't do and revenue you won't generate.

You're probably familiar with the 80/20 rule, otherwise known as the Pareto Principle. It applies to many different things, but it definitely applies to your patient base: 80 percent of your problems come from 20 percent of your patients. They cost you time and money, and they damage morale. Let's face it, if someone has canceled on you twice at the last minute, there is no way you're going to be in profit on that patient. And I can't drive this point home hard enough: *They are preventing you from treating a good patient who does respect your schedule.* Fire that patient. You'll make more money. Tell them you're going to help them find another dentist and you'll be happy to send their records to their new dentist, but you can only treat people who can respect your schedule. You are a surgical suite, not a hair salon. (And they probably never miss a hair appointment!)

What will really happen is of the 20 percent who are your problem patients, half of them will be gone (and good riddance!) and the other half will fall in line. Don't ever be afraid to lose patients. There are plenty more, and you should be earning money on each one. Plus, there is no better way to cheer your team up than to tell them that person who has been a pain in the butt for five years is no longer a patient of record. It's a gift you give yourself and your team.

Training pets and patients takes three things: time, effort, and most of all, consistency. I can un-train my dog to not beg just by giving her something from the table. It only takes once.

So decide how you want your ideal patient to behave, and reinforce that good behavior by giving them great care.

CHAPTER 33

INCONVENIENCE IS BAD MARKETING

We live in the age of convenience. We can find a nearby restaurant and make a reservation with our thumb in two minutes. We can have virtually anything delivered to our home. Uber was delivering people's Christmas trees in Manhattan last year. Amazon Prime ships for free, and it usually arrives the next day. Sometimes even on a Sunday. We can download a book, a song, a movie, or a TV show in seconds. HBO Go® and Showtime Anytime® allow you to watch any episode of any show they've ever made, anytime you want. Airplanes have Wi-Fi. The list is endless.

So when we encounter inconvenience nowadays, we are perplexed. Frustrated. Disappointed. Especially when we believe—based on everything else around us—that the possibility of convenience should exist.

The fact is, being convenient has become essential to your dental practice, and being inconvenient will stop you in your tracks. Here are the essentials.

YOUR HOURS

Have extended hours. As I mentioned previously, Saturday hours, early morning hours, and evening hours are extremely appealing nowadays. Several practices have even shifted to practicing on Sundays. This is simply a matter of accommodating your patients and knowing what the competition will do. Test the time slots and you'll see what is most desirable to your patient base. I had a practice tell me that they started opening every other Saturday, and it immediately booked out for three months. They wanted to know what they should do. Oh, I don't know…maybe open *every* Saturday? And if Saturdays book out three months in advance, that tells you something else: You might need to consider Sunday. The same would be true for evening or morning hours.

I know it can be a staffing issue. But if the dentist is not willing to adjust and find a team that will too, I can assure you that someone will eventually do it across the street from you.

Dentists will also tell me that one of the challenges with Saturdays is a higher no-show rate. So tell your patients it's a premium time in the schedule, and it has to be held with a credit card payment (which will be charged if they don't show up). Or only offer it to fee-for-service patients. Or both. There are always solutions when you're not just looking for excuses not to do something.

Convenience often comes at a price. 7-Eleven® isn't the cheapest place to buy anything. But they're open 24 hours a day (despite their name, which is now meaningless). Hertz® will now have a driver take you directly to your terminal for an extra $25 so you don't have to ride the shuttle bus. And I know many dentists who charge more for a CEREC restoration—even though it saves them money—because it's a much more convenient result. This doesn't necessarily jibe with my "be more affordable" suggestion, but hey, it's your practice. And affordability is always relative to convenience.

VOICEMAIL IS DEAD

If you're open, answer the phone. Don't EVER let it go to voicemail. People don't leave voicemails on cell phones anymore, and they don't check them, so they're going to start to do the same thing with your office voicemail. And people hang up now after the third ring. The

If you're open, answer the phone. Don't EVER let it go to voicemail.

dental industry average—which is really terrible—of letting one out of four calls go to voicemail when you're open is even more expensive than it used to be. This also goes back to my previous point about front desk staffing.

On a crazy side note, I learned that a former member of 1-800-DENTIST had a policy of letting all new patient calls go to voicemail, so that they could listen to the message and see if the patient was a good fit. They also believed that if the person was willing to leave a message, they were more likely to show up as a patient. How do you think that worked? Not only was it inconvenient, it was irrational. And it sure wasn't remarkable, at least not in a good way.

INTAKE FORMS

These should either be emailed to new patients or available for download on your website. The dream will be that they can fill them out online and it will go straight into your practice software, but the industry's not there yet.

CONVENIENT TECHNOLOGIES

Single-visit dentistry with technology like CEREC cuts treatment visits in half. Hard to get more convenient than that.

Digital radiography is easier to transmit to specialists or when the patient is changing dentists or has an out-of-town emergency.

Digital impressions get better results for the lab, are instantly transmittable, and also work for Invisalign and ClearCorrect® cases. Without the goo.

CBCT makes completing implant cases faster and more accurate, especially if it is connected to CAD/CAM technology, the way Galileos and CEREC are.

YOUR WEBSITE

Be prepared to enable your website to let existing patients make and change appointments online. I know this freaks you out, but it will be possible to do it in a secure way and not let them move their appointment to the wrong slot. This is the OpenTable® era. It has to become normal for dentistry, just as it is becoming normal for physicians and vets. The website for Aspen Dental Management®, one of the largest group practices, already offers this for all their patients—new and existing—so you can bet they won't be the last one to do it. Get ahead of the curve on this one.

Have appointment request forms on your website and Facebook as well. If you don't have the capability yet for self-serve appointing, at least do this. And respond quickly to the email that gets sent to you when the potential patient completes the form.

BEING AVAILABLE AND ACCESSIBLE

Be accessible to your patients for emergencies. Have a dedicated cell phone that one team member takes home every night, so that they can determine if the emergency merits the dentist coming in that night. That team member can also make or change appointments, as long as they can access the schedule (which should be able to be done with a phone app, by the way).

Here's a tip for your VIP patients: Give them the dentist's cell number, and let them know they can always text with a question or for an emergency. But it only works if you respond. I knew a dentist who put her mobile number on her business cards, just to show people how accessible she was. But she *never answered it!* There is no worse marketing than making a promise and not fulfilling it. She'd be better off not giving out the number at all.

DIGITAL APPOINTMENT REMINDERS AND CONFIRMATIONS

Do I really need to point out how much more convenient it is for patients to get reminders by text or email? Do you live in a cave?

Convenience is a cornerstone of a remarkable dental practice. Accept it, embrace it, and thrive with it.

CHAPTER 34

DOING THE UNEXPECTED

In *Everything is Marketing*, I discussed how you can be memorable to your patients by doing the unexpected. This is how human memory responds. Experiencing what is expected doesn't register anywhere nearly as much as something we weren't anticipating. It is often the small thing—good or bad—that sticks in our mind. You know this is true for yourself.

But now we are trying to be remarkable, which ideally translates into something shared online, reverberating your reputation. That means out-of-the-box memorable. How can you do that? Create an impression that people want to share.

Here is a perfect example of a memorable moment. One of the remarkable dentists featured in this book was running late, and a scheduled patient had to leave. The dentist called her personally that evening and apologized and told her when she was able to come in that he would give her 10 percent off the visit. How do I know this is remarkable? The patient told the story on Yelp.

It boils down to taking a few extra minutes to do something unique, personal, and unexpected that shows that you genuinely care about the person. When you approach your practice this way, you will find yourself doing remarkable things all the time.

Some other suggestions:

Treat one patient a month completely gratis. Someone in real need. Someone nominated by your team members. Obviously, you're going to post it everywhere on social media and get a video testimonial from your patient. But you're really doing it so that the whole team gets that wonderful hit of oxytocin, the hormone we secrete when we help other people selflessly. Be sure to also take a video of your team members, sharing how it feels to be able to this for someone.

Offer to do DNA storage for all of your regular patients. You could probably make a package deal with 23andMe® for less than $100 per patient. Do it as part of a prophy visit, and then log them in online so that they see what they're getting.

Do free NFL-quality mouth guards for local high school teams.

Some practices do massage, which can be a simple shoulder or scalp massage—or if your practice is large enough, you could have someone on staff.

It comes down to being inventive and creative, but also being aware in the moment what would be the most caring thing to do for that patient. That is what will be most memorable and most remarkable.

And, of course, how they experience the whole practice—subconsciously and consciously—will affect them. The greater the contrast from their negative expectations or previous dental experiences, the more they will talk about it. This often means helping people in the practice reset their attitude in the course of the day or with regard to a specific patient or activity. I have a method for that.

THE ATTITUDE REVERSAL TECHNIQUE

As I said, the practice environment is the foundation for creating the unexpected. We all are quite good at picking up the vibe of a place, often in a matter of seconds. This is a way to infuse your practice with positivity using the approach I call the Attitude Reversal Technique. I'll explain it using myself as an example.

I don't mind exercise, but for years I hated stretching. I knew it was important, but always dreaded it and often skipped it. I recently learned that stretches are most effective at the end of the workout, when your muscles are warm. So I decided to try what I call the Attitude Reversal Technique, or ART. I didn't invent the concept at all, but this is my label for it.

What I did is started telling myself the opposite of what I thought. At the beginning of my workout, I would say, "I love stretches. I can't wait to do them." I would say it out loud. And as I got close to finishing my workout, I would say to myself, "Coming up to my favorite part—stretching!" And you know what? Within a week I stopped dreading them, and by the end of two weeks I actually was looking forward to them. Now they really are my favorite part of my whole workout.

Any team member can apply ART to anything in the practice, such as:

- An incredibly cranky patient: "I can't wait to see her today! She's my favorite patient!"
- Explaining dental coverage for the 100th time: "I love getting people to understand how their coverage works!"
- Collecting money: "Every dollar we collect gets us closer to our monthly bonus—give me that phone!"

You get the idea? Hate sterilizing instruments? Fix your attitude. Hate Wednesdays? Turn hump day into jump day. Hate asking for referrals? Make a contest out of who can get the most people to respond. Whatever negativity you're generating, reverse it. This is no different than the infusing of gratefulness into the practice. Try it. You'll be amazed.

THE LAST PISTACHIO

If you like pistachios like I do, then you'll eat whatever quantity is put in front of you. Every once in a while you get one of those nasty burnt ones, and you're left furiously looking through the shells, trying to find another good one to get that rotten taste out of your mouth. But sometimes, that nasty pistachio is the last one. And it ruins the whole pound of pistachios.

This is a metaphor for the service experience. Sometimes an entire positive experience can be ruined by what happens last. Conversely, sometimes a negative experience can be fixed by what you do last. What the dentist did calling the patient that evening and apologizing for running late is a perfect example. He took the situation from negative to remarkable in two minutes.

> **Sometimes an entirely positive experience can be ruined by what happens last.**

You are in the service business, not just health care. Don't ever forget how important those last moments are. It's another reason to take care of money earlier, so it's not what the patient experiences as they're about to leave.

And saying goodbye is a big deal, because that's often the last pistachio. So make an even bigger deal out of it. Make an announcement that the patient is leaving and have a bunch of the team all come out and give a personal goodbye. Why not? Who wouldn't feel special if that happened? And how long does it take? That's why I love using walkie-talkies in a practice. You can execute maneuvers like that easily.

The entire team should understand the importance of not leaving the patient with a nasty pistachio and go out of their way to make the visit unexpected and remarkable whenever they can.

CHAPTER 35

YOUR PATIENT
INTAKE FORM

Here's a simple way to be just a little bit unique and show some of your practice personality.

You need the patient's medical history. But you need a lot more than that to create a remarkable experience. So your intake form can ask many other questions other than the pertinent medical and dental ones.

These are some suggestions. They will make it easier for you to have a more personal conversation during their visits and also be able to acknowledge special occasions in their lives. You can pick and choose from them, ignore them all and roll your eyes, or write some of your own. Most practice management software will allow you to add questions to your intake forms, but otherwise just make this a separate sheet, headed "We want to get to know you better."

- If you're married, what is your anniversary date? (You are going to send reminders on the special years.)
- What is your favorite music?
- Do you have children? Grandchildren? What are their names and ages?
- What's the worst job you ever had?
- Do you have a favorite sport?
- Who is an actor you'd like to meet?
- What languages do you speak?
- Can you wiggle your ears?
- Do you play a musical instrument?
- If you smoke, can we nag you about quitting when you come in?
- Do you have a go-to karaoke song?

Have a little fun with this. Whatever your tolerance level is.

CHAPTER 36

BEING PRESENT

The remarkable practice is not just efficient. Efficiency is what happens in the background so that everyone can be truly present when they are interacting with patients.

Many people can teach you systems and logistics to make your practice more efficient. But the most important result of those improvements should be that they allow you to focus completely on the patient you are with *at that moment*. Why is that so critical? Because we are all keenly aware when someone's attention is completely on us. It's also critical because so few people are actually present with each other these days.

And in the practice of dentistry—where anxiety, apprehension, and misinformation abound—genuine caring for the patient as an individual is even more critical. I believe it is foundational, because most patients, in order to suspend all of their irrational beliefs and behaviors regarding their oral health, have to trust you. Being present is another essential element to creating trust.

So what does "being present" really mean? And how exactly do you get there? In essence, being truly present means that when you are with a patient—whether you are the dentist, hygienist, assistant, treatment coordinator, or receptionist—your attention is 100 percent on them. You're not thinking about the next patient. Or the next piece of equipment you'd like to buy. Or that sandwich in the refrigerator calling your name. You're listening to, talking to, and focusing completely on that person.

The first step to achieving this is deciding to do it. Acknowledge that it is how you would want to be treated, and resolve to do it with everyone. Next, you need to eliminate distractions. This is a discipline in and of itself, almost like a meditation, where you do not let other thoughts interfere. And you can only do this when you have effective systems in your office, where the flow is controlled and sequenced properly, and people know their roles and complete them. It is a team effort that creates the possibility for each of you to be fully present.

It means stripping away your internal noise, or at least ignoring it, and eliminating your external noise. Interruptions are not tolerated (not even Facebook messages!). Is it easy? No. But what life skill is? As I said, the result is deep, long-term relationships grounded in trust with your patients. Otherwise, we flit from operatory to operatory, from exam to case presentation, phone call to email, always thinking about what we have to be doing next. This is how many of us live our entire lives, not in the moment, but thinking about the past or the future.

We live in a world of massive distraction, making it harder and harder to focus all the time. And, in my mind, that makes it all the more necessary. It has become so increasingly rare that when you are present, people respond to it, sensing instantly that your attention is not divided. And it's powerful.

When you are present, people respond to it, sensing instantly that your attention is not divided. That's powerful.

One of the things I like most about our training for 1-800-DENTIST call center operators is that for each call, they learn to put all their focus on that caller, forgetting about what else is going on in their lives at that moment. They forget about the frustrating call they may have just finished, and don't think about the traffic on the ride home. They are truly present for that person as an individual, with individual needs and concerns.

We train this way because we have learned it makes a huge difference when someone is trying to choose a dentist and has no idea how to make that decision.

Sound like a bunch of New Age nonsense? Okay, well from a purely business standpoint, being present is good marketing. In any service business, when a person feels someone's focused attention, they are more receptive. In your case, being more receptive means patients accepting treatment now instead of putting it off for six months or a year, or indefinitely, which doesn't benefit them or you at all. You are helping them make a good health decision, sometimes in spite of themselves, and being present is an integral part of that.

Of all the highly successful dentists I know, I can safely say that every single one of them has mastered this skill. Some came to it more naturally, but each one of them, once they saw the potency of it, made it an essential part of their practice behavior. And then built a team that behaved exactly the same way, with systems and efficiencies that all support this. And it has yielded the best kind of success: a thriving practice with healthy patients who appreciate the relationship they have with the dentists and the team.

And who knows, you may find that once you master this at work, you'll be more present with your partner, your children, your friends, and everyone you meet.

CHAPTER 37

ADAPTING TECHNOLOGY

OLD WORLD CRAFTSMAN, NEW WORLD TECHNICIAN

I've mentioned technology quite a bit throughout the book because I see digital dentistry as integral to becoming remarkable. But I still see resistance to adaptation of technology in many practices, often with systems and devices that should have been incorporated years ago.

Remarkable dentists savor their craft. They care about every detail of every procedure and hunger to do it better and faster. They strive to provide treatment more comfortably for the patient and make it last longer and look better. They also know that it isn't just their hands but their technology that makes this possible. That means they don't just learn and expand their technique, but also study and adapt new technology ahead of most of their peers, understanding that technology is always improving.

Not every dentist behaves this way. Many operate with the belief that what they learned in dental school was enough. Or once they've investigated a technology and found it unsatisfactory, they maintain that opinion for the rest of their career. But that's not reality.

The first digital camera weighed 8.5 pounds, took 30 black-and-white pictures and required a full three seconds of exposure. It was invented at Kodak in 1975. That's right—over 40 years ago. Their own inventor told them that it would take 20 years to reach consumer-level quality. Kodak executives shelved it. And now my iPhone takes a better picture than my Canon 5D and a better movie than my Sony HD video. Technology gets better.

Anyone who used CEREC 15 years ago knows it was a very technique-sensitive technology, with questionable margins and a steep learning curve. Is CEREC the same now? Of course not. The margins are as good or better than a lab, and the last lathe released improved milling time by 50 percent. And the Omnicam takes better impressions than almost every impression material available.

Digital radiography was blurry at the start, and film was much better. Did it improve? Does it give you an enormous digital image that you can use to show the patient exactly what's happening in their mouth? Clearly.

One of the keys to being remarkable is to get remarkably good results a higher percentage of the time. CAD/CAM allows you to eliminate the possibility of redoing your restorations between temporaries and final crown seating. Bear this in mind:

A study done on dental practice posts on Yelp showed that 39 percent of the reviews complained that their work had to be redone.[15] That's a big number.

There is one more critical aspect of technology—people's expectations. I ran into a dentist at a dental convention last year, and he was telling me about a patient that we had sent him. The woman was in her 30s, and spoke at length to him about her previous dentist, how wonderful he was, and how she had gone to him for years, along with most of her family.

So the dentist finally asked, "Why did you leave? Did he retire?"

"No," she said. "He just hadn't added any new technology in like 10 years, so I left and found you."

Even I found this story a little surprising, because I know how much people hate finding a new dentist. But this is how people are about technology nowadays. They don't buy a new cell phone because theirs is broken; they buy one because the new version is out and they can't stand to have the old one. They see new tech everywhere around them, and when they see a dental office that looks exactly like it did when they were 10 years old, they move on.

I'm not going to pretend to know technology from a clinical standpoint. But I do know about it from a patient perspective. Technology can be great marketing if you use it to make your dentistry more convenient and comfort conscious, and likely even more affordable, and if you communicate those benefits to your patients on a regular basis.

TECHNOLOGY MAKES DENTISTRY FUN

CAD/CAM technology to me is a cornerstone in becoming faster, better, and more affordable. But it can also reinvigorate the dentist and the team, and make doing dentistry fun and interesting.

I have spoken to many dentists who have told me that they were in the middle of their dental career and totally burned out on day-to-day dentistry, and when they added CEREC to their practice, it changed everything. It made dentistry challenging for them. It made it exciting and new, and they found they couldn't wait to get in to the office every morning. When the dentist is having fun, the team is going to be able to create that atmosphere for the patients a lot more easily.

I understand that these new technologies are expensive, and at first glance they don't seem to pay off. But is the automobile assembly robot expensive? Or does it reduce cost in the long run and very often in the short run? Are ATMs expensive? Or do they save banks hundreds of millions of dollars in teller expenses? Is Lasik technology expensive, or did it create an entirely new billion dollar marketplace? The same principle applies to many of the innovations coming to dentistry. When it is faster, more convenient, with better results, and sometimes more affordable, it is going to expand the dental marketplace, and every practice that adapts will benefit.

Consider this: Pacific Dental Services in California has more than 400 practices as of this printing, and every single one of them uses CEREC. Do they like to waste money buying toys?

I don't think so. They know their return on investment to two decimal places. In 2015, Pacific hit a milestone—they had milled their one-millionth CEREC restoration. That's impressive just from a volume standpoint, but when you think they probably saved an average of $50 per crown in lab costs, the profit sounds pretty exciting too.

I may seem biased toward CEREC, but the fact that Sirona's R&D budget for CAD/CAM dwarfs the gross *revenue* of their competitors indicates to me that they are going to stay ahead of the curve for a long time. Beyond that, new technology requires support, and they have by far the largest support workforce in this technology. Certainly their competitors are striving to make better and better technology all the time, and innovation comes from everywhere. This is just my opinion as a businessperson.

Regarding CAD/CAM and your team, there are two important aspects to consider. First and foremost, when you invest in technology like this, be sure to get buy-in from your team ahead of time. Teams seldom embrace change that is forced on them. But when presented properly—that it is about everyone growing and learning and contributing and evolving and benefitting—then the changes will be embraced, and success is almost guaranteed.

With CAD/CAM in particular, it is going to have an effect on your workflow. You will have to adapt how you all move through the practice, so it's important that the team is on board for the changes and, hopefully, excited about them. And they should be, because the second aspect is that ideally the team does most of the new steps in single-visit dentistry, and the dentist herself mostly preps the teeth and seats the crown or inlay, as she always did. Remember the three things that motivate people: responsibility, purpose, and autonomy. CEREC gives team members all three.

One of the best advantages to technology like CEREC is that it virtually eliminates redos based on failed impressions or lab mistakes. No patient wants work redone. And even if it was the lab's fault, the patient doesn't really care. They don't want two visits to finish that crown, never mind three. And the blame falls on you and is not remarkable to anyone.

There is a wide range of new technology available to you now, from soft tissue lasers to electric hand pieces, and of course digital radiography. But from a standpoint of the expanding marketplace of dental implants, cone beam technology is perhaps the most revolutionary. CBCT gets results more quickly, with less surgery, and with a much higher degree of accuracy. Sounds remarkable to me.

Even I can understand that, clinically, there is a vast difference between two-dimensional images and three dimensional. The capability for precision is exponentially better. And when you combine technology like GALILEOS and CEREC, your ability to deliver incredibly accurate implants in a single visit is vastly enhanced. This is a perfect example of what I mean about expanding the dental marketplace with convenience.

On the other side of the coin is the risk involved in not using CBCT when placing implants today. The litigation for failed implants can be staggeringly expensive. There have been settlements in the hundreds of thousands dollars. And when you have placed implants without 3-D imaging and had a subsequent negative result, your position is almost indefensible. To me the clinical benefit coupled with the reduced risk makes use of this technology essential.

SLOW DOWN TO SPEED UP

More than one dentist has told me that the reason they haven't made the move to CAD/CAM is because it will slow them down. But this is the reality with learning anything new, or adapting to very different technology. Even something as simple as learning to type required that you first had to write slower than you did by hand until you got significantly faster (and more legible!) as your typing skills improved. This is the basic paradigm for growth: You have to be willing to slow down temporarily so that you can speed up permanently.

The whole team needs to accept this reality of improvement. It may cost you a little money and time, but with team commitment and the right training and guidance, you can shorten the learning cycle considerably.

The purchase of technology always involves calculations of your return on investment. And with proper guidance, the ROI is there, because you are not going to be the first practice to use these technologies. The successful pathway has already been paved. With coaching and training, a CEREC is an ATM machine. But staging and adapting new technology in the right order is important. You can do too much at once, just as you can fall behind the curve. But great technology is out there, improving every day, and patients are expecting it.

Great technology exists and is improving every day—and patients are expecting it.

When considering new tech, be sure to factor in the marketing value of the technology as well as your ability to deliver better dentistry. It is important to factor in the less tangible but often more critical aspect of the patient experience. If you fail to incorporate this into your calculation, believing that everything can be reduced to a dollars-and-cents assessment, I will remind you that you are in a subjective health care profession.

And once you have it, talk about it. Do office tours for new patients, and include all your great technology, with a layman's explanation of the benefits to the patients. Your website and all social media should include explanations and videos, and your newsletters should continually feature the advanced levels of technology that you offer. That maximizes the value of the technology and loads the patient's mind with what to say when promoting you to the world because you are so amazing and unique.

We are at a point in technological evolution where adding to and upgrading your systems has to become part of your annual budget. This is much more manageable when you have escaped gravity in your practice, but no matter what, it has to be integrated into your growth plan.

SECTION SIX:

PRACTICAL
TOOLS

REMARKABLE DENTIST #5

Brian Toorani, DDS
Dental Oasis of Orange County
Huntington Beach, CA
dentaloasisofoc.com
facebook.com/dentaloasis1

Year opened: 2006

REMARKABLE NUMBERS:

Annual revenue: $1.5 million
Gross profit margin: 35 percent
Associates: 1
New patients per month: 25; 80 percent from referrals

REMARKABLE STORY:

It was July 2, 2010, and Brian Toorani had hit rock
bottom. He had $22 in his checking account and was
drowning in debt. He had tried to cut expenses, but he
was realizing that cost-cutting didn't create growth.

Sitting down with his wife to sort out their future, he
suddenly remembered he had $6,000 worth of Visa® gift
cards he had purchased to reward patients for referring,

but due to California regulations could no longer use them for that purpose. So that's what his family lived on for three months, while he made one big bet on his future.

That bet was buying a CEREC. Desperately needing to cut his lab bill, he watched dozens of training videos and did 20 restorations in the first week. In the first month he reduced his lab bill by $7,000, and by the second month he cut it completely.

Within 19 months he paid off the CEREC loan, plus his whole distributor debt. He discovered that he could do more dentistry, faster, and that the patients loved it.

Now, believing in the impact of technology on his patients and his productivity, he added GALILEOS in 2012, and it has vastly expanded his capabilities and accuracy.

REMARKABLE QUOTE:

"We don't come to work to do dentistry, we come to see our friends who happen to need dentistry."

WHAT PEOPLE SAY:

"Beyond the best experience ever. The fact that my 7-year-old drama queen was upset to *leave* the office made my year!"

"After writing what I would call a fair, but not so flattering review of Dental Oasis, I received a call from Dr. Toorani himself, He was concerned about my negative experience and wanted the opportunity to give me a better experience. At no time did he ask me to change my star review. He apologized for the unpleasant experience and asked me to give them one more try. I took him up on the offer. I had my appointment yesterday with him and from beginning to end the experience was excellent."

[Fred says: "Now that's how to fix a negative review. And then there's this one:"]

"I call him Superman!"

CHAPTER 38

MAKE THE BREAD,
BUY THE BUTTER

This chapter's title is also the title of a cookbook by Jennifer Reese. She has done all sorts of research to basically see what makes sense for all different types of cooking—doing it yourself or letting someone better do it. I think it's a great principle to apply to any business. With all the systems and processes in your practice, ask yourself: What are you doing that you shouldn't be doing yourself, and what are you *not* doing yourself that you *should be*?

Focus on those things that only you and your team can do well, and outsource those things that can be done cheaper or better by someone else.

Is it costing you more to do it yourself? Are you doing it so inefficiently that you are losing money in the process? Is there a faster, more cost-effective way for someone else to do it, freeing up time for you to deliver dentistry (which, after all, is why you're there)? A great office manager is always looking for ways to do this and is calculating the time/value ratio for you. A not-so-great office manager is trying to keep everything inside—under her control—so she has job security. The same goes for the dentist. Is she doing all the social media updates herself? That won't prep a tooth. Delegate and outsource for efficiency. And focus and refine your skills with those things that you should be doing or do better than anyone else.

Focus on those things that only you can do, or you and your team can do well, and outsource those things that can be done cheaper or better by someone else.

For example, does the dentist sign the checks, or is someone else paying bills and charging to company credit cards without your approval or oversight? As I mentioned in Chapter 25, embezzlement only happens when you don't have knowledge and control of your money. I know businesses doing $40 million a year where the owners still sign all the checks except for payroll, and that require two signatures for anything over $3,000. Sign your own checks, and have checks and balances set up so that no one person controls everything. A remarkable practice cultivates an environment of trust, but I also preach the concept of "lead them not into temptation."

Along those same lines, compliance with employment law is harder than ever, particularly if you live in states like California. It's very challenging for any small business to stay ahead of all the regulations, and the risk of employee lawsuits goes up all the time, as do the fines from state and local entities when you are violating statutes. My advice is to outsource all that to a company like HR for Health. You can even include your payroll and employee evaluations, plus access a lot of time-saving features while radically reducing your exposure and risk.

And please don't tell me you're doing your own taxes. There are CPAs that specialize in dentistry. They know your business, and they know it relative to other practices as well. They can tell you when you are above the norm on expenses and what you should be reserving for taxes. And they should save you enough on your annual tax filings that they are essentially a free service. I've paid my personal accountant $1,500 a year to do my taxes for decades. He's saved me hundreds of thousands at this point. There are two main societies of dental CPAs listed in the *Resources* section.

Are you doing insurance billing yourself? This has become one of the great time-sucks in a practice—and if you don't do it right, you don't get paid. That's a pretty big penalty for failure, and I'm sure you've also noticed that insurance companies are working to make it harder and harder for you to get less and less reimbursement. Let claims age too long and you could lose the money entirely. Outsource this, and like any good service, it should pay for itself and then some. Look into DentalBilling.com or Virtual Dental Office in the *Resources* section.

Most of the advertising that you do should probably be done by an outside resource. It is unlikely that you have the skills to buy Google AdWords effectively, or plan a direct marketing campaign, or build your own website. As long as you track the results of your promotions yourself, and make the budget decisions accordingly, your time will be better spent delivering dentistry.

As a general dentist, as you expand your skills and services, you will be doing more endo, clear aligner ortho, and simpler implant cases, all of which I recommend—but you should always be making sure that the patient is not being under-served. If the case is a stretch for you, err on the side of caution and refer it out. You owe that to your patients, and it will pay off in the long run. Don't get seduced by the chance to do a high-profit procedure that could lead to failure or require redoing by a specialist. Litigation may ensue, and your reputation will suffer, and the short-term gain will turn into a long-term loss.

Do right by your patients, and there will always be enough work. Specialists exist for a reason. And if you are a specialist, don't resent GPs for doing more work themselves. Just be there for the larger and more complex cases, and be willing to consult with them and advise them on the smaller ones. That way everyone wins, especially the patients.

There are software applications and services that can do things faster, better, and cheaper than you can do them yourself. Buy the butter, so to speak—that way you can concentrate on making a lot more bread.

THE TRAP OF SUNK COSTS

There is a corollary to this thinking, and it applies to the concept of sunk costs. A sunk cost is something you have already made the investment in. The money is spent, and sometimes the investment turns out to be wrong, of low value, or as often happens, a better solution comes along. The mistake many

businesspeople make is to cling to the investment either because it was expensive or they harbor the fantasy that they can
still extract some value.

Let me give you an example. Let's say that five years ago you
spent $12,000 with a website company building an elaborate,
beautiful, well-optimized new website for your practice. After
all these years, you now realize that this website has become
technologically outdated, and you're watching your ranking in
search results drop and drop. In short, you need a new website.
But you already paid *$12,000 for the last one!* It's too painful
to scrap it and pay for another one. This is the trap of the sunk
cost in a nutshell.

The smart businessperson knows that trying to milk a fraction of the value of a sunk cost is a waste of time and prevents
growth. If you bought a custom chair that made your back
hurt all the time, the day you get a new chair that stopped the
pain, you'd realize that you had been clinging to a sunk cost to
your own detriment.

Dentists agonize over these types of investments all the time.
All it does is slow you down. It could be technology, it could
be software, or it could be a team member. Free yourself from
the trap. Invest in the better solution, and don't look back.

CHAPTER 39

THE FUTURE
OF WEBSITES

My first book goes into great detail about practice websites, so I'll just remind you of two key facts:

1. Patients will judge the quality of your dentistry by the quality of your website. I know that these two things are unrelated in your case, but with respect to most other businesses, consumers can get a sense of the service, product, or company by the website. So people transfer that general rule to you.

2. Patients check three main resources when looking for a dentist: the practice website, social media, and online review sites. Many times, they will check all three, because it's so easy to do. They can do it all on their mobile phone.

Your website is the hub around which all your promotion will revolve, as the searcher is likely to end up there to make their final decision. Consumers are doing this even after they've gotten a recommendation from a friend. And if they don't see an appealing website, the judgment will not be in your favor.

Your website needs to be dynamic, which means something very specific in the digital world. It means that you can change the content easily yourself, adding photos, video, and text whenever you want, almost like a Facebook page. And it also means that you can have additional content like patient reviews feeding automatically to your website.

You are serving two masters with your website: the consumer and Google. The consumer wants relevant results in a clean, clear format. Google wants to see relevant, ever-changing content. A dynamic website is the only way to solve this.

Some dentists will tell me that they spent $10,000-$12,000 building a custom website a few years ago, and it should be fine, even though they can't change the content without paying their webmaster to do it. It's not fine. Remember my discussion about sunk costs? It doesn't matter what you paid if it doesn't serve your needs anymore. Let it go.

WEBSITE ESSENTIALS

APPOINTMENT REQUEST FORM

As I mentioned earlier, patients need to be able to request an appointment right there on your website. (This is the age of instant gratification, remember?) It should send an email to your receptionist or office manager and, hopefully, get a quick reply. Until you can have a self-serve appointing module there, this is the best you can do, but you need to do it.

MOBILE VERSION

Sixty percent of Internet searches start on mobile phones.[16] With dental practices, more people will eventually go to a larger device, but you still absolutely need a specific mobile version, called a responsive version, which reformats to fit smart phones. And it's not just the consumer that will judge you harshly—it's now Google. As of April 2015, the company was very clear that not having a responsive mobile website that loads quickly will significantly hurt your ranking. Make sure this is what your site does, or fix it immediately.

FINANCING APPLICATION

Cost is always an issue with patients, and knowing that you offer financing, and that they can apply right there on your website, is a huge and appealing benefit. CareCredit® will even help you put a payment calculator right on your website.

REVIEWS PAGE

You need a separate page on your site for patient reviews. I don't mean written testimonials from your patients that you've edited. Those have almost no credibility in the age of online reviews. You need several types of reviews, including video, survey-generated and Yelp reviews. The last two should feed automatically into your website. Wait, did I say have your Yelp reviews appear in your website? Yes. Because when the consumer decides to leave and go to Yelp, searches your name and finds your profile, they will see ads for 13 other dentists, unless you are a paid advertiser on Yelp. You will lose potential patients this way. It also shows your confidence and transparency that you are willing to put the unvarnished reviews from Yelp right there in your own website. Unfortunately, you can't currently do this with Google reviews.

Then you need the reviews generated by your automated communication application—PatientActivator, RevenueWell®, DemandForce® or some other system that surveys your patients and gathers reviews—to be fed automatically to your website, giving you that precious ever-changing content. Remember, both the consumer and Google like to see real reviews. And only a dynamic website can do this.

Lastly, you need video reviews, which I'll cover in the next chapter in more detail. But let's talk first about what all the SEO experts are trying to sell you.

THE MYTH OF THE FIRST PAGE GUARANTEE

Most likely, if your website is more than two or three years old, it needs a serious refresh, if not a total redo. And there are a lot of website companies out there willing to build you a site and "guarantee" to get you on the first page in a Google search.

There are a number of reasons why this promise is a false one, but the primary reason is this: When someone searches "dentist 90049," for example, the first thing Google offers is three paid ads at the top. Then it will show a map and a list of seven more dentists, and after that you can scroll down and see up to seven more (many of which are repeats from the map). So in any given ZIP code, Google is only going to present between 10 and 12 dentists on the first page who are not paying to be there—appearing "organically," as the terminology goes.

So when 80 percent of dentists have a website, is it really possible for them <u>all</u> to appear on the first page? And can someone rework your SEO to such a degree that you will be guaranteed to appear there? What if they have 15 clients in that ZIP code, or there are 15 SEO "experts" all guaranteeing first page results? What happens then? I think you know.

And wait, there's another important factor to consider. **Google gives different results to different people based on their previous search history.** In other words, you could be sitting there on your laptop and do a search for "comedy clubs in Baltimore," and your spouse could be sitting next to you using an iPad doing the exact same search, and you would get two different results.

That's because Google has built a profile on you based on your previous searches and tries to decide what your preferences might be. Their goal is to give the best possible result for *you*— and they have a number of tricks to figure that out. This is not unlike what Amazon does, offering you recommendations based on what you previously bought and viewed.

The fact is that Google gives search results based on anywhere from 400-800 bits of information—much of it variable—but most of them Google does not tell us, as they don't want less-than-honest companies "gaming" the search and stealing the clicks. Also, different devices and browsers affect results. For example, if you use Google Chrome, it's looking at your Google+ page to see what you posted, shared, and commented on relative to that search. All in milliseconds, of course.

So what does that "expert" mean when he makes this first page promise? He means that he can get you to appear on the first page of Google on one computer, one time, and he is going to take a screen shot to show you that it happened, so he can bill you for the website and keep your money.

Why do these people promise this? Because that's what dentists tell them they want. Of course. Who doesn't want to be on the first page? But when most of the dentists in your area have a website, you're not all going to get on the first page, unless the screen is the size of a movie theater screen. And even if you do appear today on the first page, it won't mean you'll be there tomorrow. Or an hour from now.

Even if you do appear today on the first page, it won't mean you'll be there tomorrow. Or an hour from now.

So what's a dentist to do? The operative principle is to have truly relevant, *ever-changing* content on a website that is visually appealing and easy to navigate. Then, as people get more and more sophisticated in their searching, they are going to put in more detail in the search box. So, for example, instead of searching for "dentist Spokane," they will search "dentist 99026 Saturday hours reviews CEREC" and get a much more refined SERP. (SERP stands for "search engine results page," which is an acronym you will start to see more and more.)

This will mean that the more relevant, precise content you have in your website, the more Google will be able to offer you as a first page result when people get this specific. Websites will always be a bit of a moving target, but having a dynamic one makes it possible for you to adapt to those changes a lot more quickly and less expensively.

Go to any of the remarkable dentists' websites and you'll see it done well.

239

CHAPTER 40

THE ULTIMATE MARKETING TOOL: VIDEOS

Video rules.

Who rules it? Well, in April 2015 YouTube was averaging 7 billion views a day. But Facebook had 4 billion and is on track to overtake YouTube.[17] It already dominates the highest-viewed videos, having the top five. What this means is people love to watch and really love to share videos.

And consumers are five times more likely to watch a video than read content in its entirety.[18] That's pretty easy to believe in the world of Twitter's 140 character communications.

When it comes to your practice marketing, videos are gold and have more uses than any other promotional content.

Why is Facebook catching up so fast in video views? Because people check into Facebook constantly, unlike YouTube. And they share what they like with all their friends with just two clicks. And in case you haven't noticed, videos start playing automatically on Facebook as you reach them scrolling on your wall. (If that's all gibberish to you, don't worry—we'll be assigning social media to someone else on your team.)

In terms of your practice, videos come in two types: testimonials from patients, and the dentist and practice showcase. And they have many differences.

PATIENT TESTIMONIALS

These are short, simple, one-take videos, shot with a smart phone for easy uploading.

DENTIST/PRACTICE SHOWCASE

These are well-produced, scripted videos. One is the tour of the practice, sometimes inserted with interviews of patients. The other is the dentist talking directly to camera, introducing her practice and sharing her practice philosophy. These are done with the help of professionals.

For the showcase videos, you should use a professional video company like those I mention in the *Resources* section. But I'm going to focus on the patient videos.

As I mentioned earlier, written, edited-down, and cherry-picked testimonials from patients are only slightly more credible than reviewers' comments in movie ads. But a simple video of a patient talking about why they like their dentist is extremely powerful. And one of the reasons they are not meant to be highly produced or staged or scripted is because the more real and genuine they are, the more believable they are.

That also means it's really easy to do them. So do lots of them—with all different types of patients, because we like to get advice from people we identify with. The more variety in the people you have videos of, the more appealing you will be to a large audience of potential patients. We want someone our age, our gender, and very often our ethnicity to be most comfortable. We're human, after all. A wide spectrum of patients is what works best.

These are the steps to making patient testimonial videos:

1. Ask a patient if she would be willing to do a quick video about being a patient. Many people will be concerned that they won't do a good job or look good, so just say, "If you don't like it, we'll delete it. But we're just looking for 30 seconds in your own words."
2. Use a smart phone, and record the video in horizontal mode (landscape, it's often called).
3. Say to the patient, "Just tell us what it's like to be a patient of ours."
4. Retake it if they're not happy with it. But you'll be amazed what people will say when speaking from the heart, and most often the first time is the best. Don't

do it over and over. The naturalness of the person is a big part of what is persuasive. Don't worry about making it perfect.

5. Get a release from the patient to use it in all media in perpetuity. (You should have this kind of release for all your patients anyway. See the *Resources* section.)

6. Post it everywhere.

This is where you can post these videos:

- Your website
- Your YouTube Channel
- Your Google+ practice profile
- Your Yelp practice profile
- Your Facebook practice page
- Twitter
- Instagram

Be sure to tag the video properly with hashtags on Facebook, Instagram, and Twitter, and tags on YouTube. If you haven't claimed your business on these sites and are not active in them, then you are behind the eight ball on this and need to get on it immediately. The *Resources* section tells you where to do it.

Jack Hadley, whose company, My Social Practice, does brilliant work in social media, suggests that you use the patient's phone to do the video (or even just to take a picture), because then it's even easier for the patient to post herself. Have her email it to you, and then you can use it also and share it and post it everywhere. Jack is seldom wrong when it comes to social media.

As you can see, videos have amazing utility for promotion. I also highly recommend that you show them to your team in the daily or weekly huddle to remind them of how much people really do appreciate what you do, even though they don't always verbalize it. Try to do one video a week.

The Remarkable Dentists listed in this book do excellent patient and practice videos. Check out their Facebook pages and YouTube to see them.

CHAPTER 41

YOUR COMPREHENSIVE SOCIAL MEDIA STRATEGY

Twenty-five percent of consumers say they would be willing to find a dentist on Facebook. Seventy-four percent of them say they are influenced by online reviews. Seventy million photos a day are shared on Instagram. Americans average 37 minutes a day on social media. In short, you need a comprehensive strategy for dealing with the digital world in order to capitalize on how remarkable your practice is.

So where should your time, energy, and money go?

Facebook is the dominant force in social media. In fact, Google+ is currently repurposing itself, essentially forfeiting the match with Facebook as a social media resource. And patients find Facebook more credible—they trust Facebook recommendations three times more than Yelp reviews. Which makes sense, because it's their friends, or friends of friends, making recommendations, not strangers. Which is not to minimize Yelp's impact. It's significant, and ever-growing. Users post more than 27,000 reviews every *minute!* It has over 100 million unique visitors in a month in the US.[19] It's a monster.

Look at it this way: Social media is your new signage. And it's on 24 hours a day, so you need to be present in as many places as possible, because people use multiple applications, and you want to be found wherever they are.

You need a three-pronged approach:

- Generating reviews on an ongoing basis
- Posting on social media multiple times a week
- Monitoring, replying, and sharing across all media

To accomplish this, you need to assign someone in the practice to do this as part of her job. I affectionately call this person the "Facebook Geek." Generally, everyone already knows who that person is. It should *not* be one of the dentists. They have clinical responsibilities. This should involve 15-30 minutes a day, with a specific set of goals and responsibilities.

GENERATING PATIENT REVIEWS

This is paramount. You need a steady stream of patient reviews being posted on Yelp and Google. And you need surveys going out to each patient after his or her visit so that you can post reviews they may write to your website and on social media.

Software like PatientActivator, RevenueWell, etc., helps you do all this.

The primary way to ask for Google and Yelp reviews is through email. Email a patient with a request for a review, and have a link within that email that leads them directly to your profile in Yelp or Google. You need to make it as easy as possible for the patient to do this. And don't expect all of them to do it. If you get one good review a week for each site that's fantastic.

You also don't want to send these emails out all at once. Meter them out on a steady basis, because it looks much better to have a review or two a week than 30 in three days.

With respect to Google, only a person with a gmail address can write a review, so this makes it easy to select which patients to send the email. Send the Yelp request to everyone else. Your software should allow you to build a list of people, and then the Facebook Geek sends out 20 or 30 a week.

You will also get some written comments from your patient surveys that go out automatically. Usually with one click you can post the good ones to social media, and with a dynamic website you can have them appear on your reviews page automatically. Unfortunately, there is no way for you to directly post these yourself on Yelp or Google.

However, what you can do when a patient writes a particularly juicy one is copy that review and include the text in an email to the patient, requesting they do a Yelp or Google review. Say, "We really appreciate you doing this review for us and would love it if you could just copy it and post it to our Google/Yelp profile by clicking this link." (This would be a personal email from the practice, not part of the batch emails you'd be sending.)

With Yelp, there is an extra challenge in that they "filter" good reviews—which is to say, they hide them—unless you are an advertiser, apparently. This is especially true for Yelp users who have posted only a few reviews, as Yelp considers them suspect. What you are looking for is a patient who has done more than 25 reviews on Yelp, as that person's review will most likely not be filtered. It's an unfortunate reality, and many people have tried and failed to litigate this with Yelp. I recommend doing what it takes to get an abundance of good reviews and not worry about anything else.

The suggested ratio of good reviews to bad is 7:1, so if you've got people writing negative reviews, you want to combat that with positivity, as well as the strategy laid out in *Appendix II* for getting the patient to take it down.

As I mentioned in the website section, you need a reviews page on your site where your automated reviews and Yelp reviews can appear, and this would be the same page where you would have patient testimonial videos. Yelp controls which reviews appear, and it will only display three, but it keeps people on your website.

I don't recommend spending any real time on other review sites like HealthGrades or Angie's List. Patients may post there on their own, and that's fine, but I suggest you focus on where the main audience is.

POSTING ON SOCIAL MEDIA

Facebook. This is where the action is. This site has the most daily users, and it's where people spend most of their time. They check it when they wake up, throughout the day, and before they go to bed. And it's only getting bigger and broader in its impact, just as it did roaring into the video market and overtaking the powerhouse YouTube in a shockingly short amount of time.

Your goal on Facebook will be to post consistently, at least a couple of times a week. This is not the place for clinical posts. It is where people are going to learn how patients feel about being in your practice, what type of experience they can expect, and the spirit of your office. There can be some dental advice, but it should be very basic.

Instagram. Even though it is now bigger than Twitter in terms of active users, this is still primarily a photo sharing site, and it doesn't have the same level of engagement or value for businesses like dental practices. But that will change, so keep an eye on it.

Twitter. Some people will tell you that there is the potential for good action on Twitter for dental practices. I don't believe this is true relative to the amount of time it takes. You would need to generate a lot of Twitter followers—your patients— and you're already trying to get them to like you on Facebook and write reviews for you. Don't squander their willingness to help by spreading it too thin. You can post there, but mostly the Facebook Geek is replicating what she posted elsewhere, or linking to it, and that is mostly for the SEO value.

LinkedIn. This is another site that doesn't serve dental practices well, in my experience. It is much more of a business-to-business environment, which it does very well.

Google+. As I said, Google is virtually abandoning its social media approach here and moving in another direction. But you *absolutely* still need a Google profile, chock full of relevant information and a verified Google+ page, as that is going to show up in a search, as is the number of Google reviews you have.

Bear in mind also that a majority of the time spent on all these sites is on smart phones.

This should go without saying: Don't violate HIPAA! Watch what you say about treatment when you show a patient and identify them. And again, make sure you're getting a release from any patient who you use an image or video of. You should have one for all the practice employees as well.

What to post:

- Photos of happy patients who've finished cases
- Happy patient of the week
- Special events the practice participates in, such as local charities
- Holiday images
- Before-and-after images
- Dental-related public interest articles
- Team outings
- Random fun photos unrelated to dentistry
- Patient reviews

- Cartoons that are dental-related
- Contests
- Selfies of dentists or team members and patients
- Promotions, like holiday whitening discounts or free implant exams

If you want to see Facebook done well, check out the practice pages of the Remarkable Dentists.

MONITORING, RESPONDING, AND SHARING

These all fall into the responsibilities of the Facebook Geek, with some recourse to the dentist with respect to negative reviews.

THE DUTIES OF THE FACEBOOK GEEK:

- Getting likes on Facebook from patients
- Checking and responding to reviews on Yelp (the negative ones should be shown to the dentist to resolve)
- Monitoring everything written about the practice across the Internet
- Posting, sharing, and responding on Facebook
- Mirroring Facebook posts on Twitter and LinkedIn
- Systematically requesting written Google and Yelp reviews from patients
- Posting automated reviews to Facebook and Twitter
- Soliciting video testimonials from patients and posting them in all the appropriate places

- Including hashtags and tags on all images, posts, and videos
- Finding interesting and amusing articles, images, and cartoons on other pages to share
- Making sure there is a signed release from any patient whose image or video is being used

The best tool available to the Facebook Geek is an automated communication application like DemandForce, RevenueWell, or PatientActivator, which will facilitate emailing to patients and also generate reviews from surveys. A second key tool is a product like ReputationMonitor, which scans the entire Internet for any mention of the dentist or practice, whether it's on social media, review sites, or directory sites, and brings them all into one dashboard. ReputationMonitor will also send an alert anytime a Yelp or Google review has been posted.

Please keep in mind that digital media is a fast-moving target. It's almost impossible for me to write accurately in this book about it because by the time the ink is dry, Facebook or Google has changed something. So the last part of the Facebook Geek's job is to stay current—which means reading blogs like mine (GoAskFred.com) and taking courses at annual meetings to keep abreast of the ever-changing environment.

CHAPTER 42

WHAT TO SPEND
ON ADVERTISING

When most dentists ask me about this, they usually are trying to determine what percentage of their revenue should be allocated to advertising, often worrying that they are spending too much. My answer is that it's more likely that they're not spending enough or that they're spending it in the wrong places.

First, let me say that in order to answer this question, you have to be tracking the results of all your advertising. You need to know where patients come from, and this can be done primarily by making sure that the source of each patient—either some promotion or a referral from an existing patient—is entered in your software so that you can run a production report.

> **If you're not tracking the results of all your advertising, you're guessing.**

But let's get back to the main question. There are only two reasons why you might be spending too much *overall* on advertising and promotion:

1. Your schedule is full for the next three to six weeks. If you can't see new patients within two or three days at the most, then you will be wasting money on advertising.
2. Word of mouth is not your number one source of new patients. This is the clearest indicator that the experience of being one of your patients does not inspire people to recommend you, and you need to fix that. You are not anywhere near remarkable enough.

As far as your advertising budget, there are two ways to look at it: as a dollar amount or as a percentage of your annual revenue.

As a rule of thumb, 5 percent of your annual revenue is a reasonable amount to spend on your advertising. I know thriving practices that spend as high as 8 percent because they know that their profitability is higher once they have paid their fixed expenses—they've escaped gravity—so they can afford to invest in growth.

As a dollar amount, your marketing costs should range from $20,000 to $40,000 per year. This would be higher with a startup practice—perhaps double that amount—because you need to start building a patient base, and every empty slot in your schedule is killing you. You need to *have* patients to be able to generate word-of-mouth patients.

Here is how I would break down the spending:

1. Your Website. This is the cornerstone of your practice promotion. Even word-of-mouth patients are likely to visit your website before calling the practice. And this is important to remember—*your website is a work in progress.* It's never done, because Google is looking every day at it, seeing what has changed. If your website hasn't changed in three years, or it's not dynamic, you need a new one pronto.

Cost: $3,000-5,000 for a new website, $75 per month or less to host and maintain it. Also, heavy duty SEO will cost thousands more, some of it monthly.

2. Social Media. This is primarily a marketing cost. This cost is part of the Facebook Geek's pay, assuming 12-15 hours a month dedicated to this. There are outside services that can do this, but you would still need someone on your team monitoring their activities.

Cost: $250-300 per month.

3. Discounts. Realize that this is part of your marketing cost. If you're doing a free exam, cleaning, and X-rays, the cost may not be high—especially if you have digital radiography—but it's not nothing. You still have to pay your hygienist.

Cost: $300-500 per month, assuming 10 new patients attracted this way.

4. Insurance plans. Dentists often forget that this is a marketing cost, too. You are discounting your work to attract patients through the plan. This number is impossible for me to estimate for you, but I want you to be mindful of it as a promotional expense. And you can calculate it fairly easily, since you know what you collect versus what you would have.

5. Advertising. This could be anything from bidding on Ad-Words to advertising on Yelp or Facebook, doing direct mail, local newspaper ads, or even radio or TV. Or referral programs like 1-800-DENTIST.

Cost: $1,000 to $5,000 per month.

When it comes to advertising, I believe in doing everything that works. Keep in mind that the lifetime value of a new patient to your practice is substantial, and it's worth investing in. Billboards and ValPak® may work in your neighborhood, even if they don't work in others. Have experimental money to spend, and track what happens.

With Google AdWords, it all depends on how much other dentists are bidding in your area. I believe in outsourcing this, but be aware that the provider is merely choosing the same keywords that you would and keeping some of the money that would go toward buying clicks, so choose someone reputable. Often this can be handled by your website provider. This is the most reliable way to drive people to your website.

Facebook is coming around in terms of the value of the ads, so I would start experimenting with it. And if it doesn't yield, try again next year.

Yelp advertising is also very dependent on your neighborhood, as it is used much more heavily in urban areas right now. But it is expanding around the country at a rapid pace, and there is the other added benefit of your good reviews suddenly appearing instead of being filtered.

Other factors that would increase your advertising cost:

- You don't have storefront visibility to your practice, which could add 20 percent or more to your budget.
- You have limited hours or less convenient hours than your local competitors.
- You don't take any emergency patients.
- Your front desk team is not strong at bringing new patients in.

In short, anything that limits the convenience and appeal to a new patient is going to diminish your results, making advertising more expensive.

Advertising as an industry is changing at a dizzying pace, and it's all any of us can do to keep up. Get professional help.

You could also be spending too much on a particular marketing approach. Every medium will have diminishing results eventually, either as you increase the budget to too high a level, or over the course of time. Direct mail, for example, will almost always oversaturate a market eventually and you'll need to stop for a few months. (1-800-DENTIST would be an exception because we're constantly modifying our advertising approach to compensate for this.)

You could also be using a promotional approach that gets lots of calls, but has very little conversion into real patients, or yields low production. If you're getting the wrong type of patients, it means either the message is wrong, you aimed at the wrong target audience, or the medium is wrong. I considered Groupon® a classic example of this, and though a few people made it work, I'm glad it's faded away from the dental world.

My main suggestion is to get professional help. Advertising as an industry is changing at a dizzying pace, and it's all any of us can do to keep up. And get someone who works in the dental industry. Consumers behave very differently when it comes to dentistry (in case you haven't noticed!), and you want a resource that understands that.

A good practice consultant, as well as your products distributor rep, should both be resources for you to find the best help and to make sure you're getting the best results.

With advertising, it's also important to manage your expectations and understand how that world works.

IT'S A NUMBERS GAME

What most of us in the advertising world have come to know is that nothing yields 100 percent results. And most small business people who operate in a sales environment know that for every 100 phone calls they make, for example, they are going to get 5-10 real prospects and maybe one new client. So they don't have an expectation that every interaction or response is going to yield new business.

It's hard for dentists to adapt to this kind of thinking because they work in health care, which is not technically a sales-oriented environment, unless you're a dermatologist or a cosmetic surgeon. But certainly any business that does advertising and has elective or optional services involves some sales—a point I've made many times about dentistry—and so it's important also to adjust your expectations and measurements away from 100 percent success.

For example, if you do online advertising and it gets 10 patients to appoint, and 80 percent of those patients actually show up for their appointment, that's a good result. And if 80 percent of those patients accept treatment, that's also a good result. The cost is also a factor. If the advertising to attract those 10 appointments was only $600, then it was an excellent result. If it was $6,000, it wasn't.

The main reason I'm recommending this viewpoint is I don't want you to miss out on good patients because you've tried some type of advertising that in your mind didn't work, but from a real-world numbers standpoint did well. This means you need to have a clear understanding of patient value.

NEW PATIENT VALUE

What should you be willing to spend to get a new patient? I discussed this in detail in *Everything is Marketing,* so I'll simplify the calculation. If a new patient is worth $10,000 over the life of the practice—a conservative number if you do even limited implants—and that patient refers five more patients to the practice over the course of five years, what would you be willing to pay to get that patient?

If I said that you should be willing to spend $1,000 to get a new patient, you'd tell me I was nuts. But from a numbers standpoint, that new patient is worth up to $60,000 in production when you consider the five new patients he brings. That means your advertising cost was less than 2 percent on that production. Doesn't sound so nuts anymore, does it? Granted, not every patient yields that much, but you can do this calculation yourself and plug in whatever you think the most conservative number is. But I believe if you are a remarkable dentist, that new patient is going to bring even more than five new patients to the practice.

Part of the problem is that dentists use $0 as the baseline measurement. They'll compare the cost of a new patient from advertising to a word-of-mouth referral, which cost them nothing. But that isn't how businesses really calculate marketing costs. They look at it relative to other paid sources of new clients—and I'm suggesting you look at it the same way, as an investment in the growth of your business. The reality is, almost any type of dental advertising, if it's worth anything and done right, is not going to cost you anywhere near $1,000 a patient. And the long-term production value of a patient is one of the huge advantages of a dental practice.

Now you might be saying, "Yes, but my overhead on that $60,000 is 75 percent." Is it? Have you not escaped gravity? Because if you haven't, then all the more reason to invest in your growth until you reverse that margin so all new business is 80 percent profit.

So stop using $0 as your baseline. Word of mouth does not count in the calculation, except in the value that new patient brings. All you want to do is attract patients within a reasonable range of cost. So what's reasonable for you?

Here's a different way to calculate it, a rule of thumb version.

I know that every area of the country is different, and often every practice is different in terms of what you charge (and what insurance reimburses). So the range of what you should be willing to pay in advertising for a new patient varies accordingly. So let's measure it as a percentage of your crown cost. If you get an average of $1,000 for a crown, you should be willing to pay 40 percent of that for a new patient in your area, or $400. If you only get $700 for a crown, the reasonable cost should be $280.

Another way to calculate this is to look at what practices are selling for in your area. Take a practice selling for $750,000, with an average of 1,000 active patients. About 25 percent of those patients will not continue with the new dentist, on average. That equals 750 real patients. Which means $1,000 per patient record. Assume the facility is half the value of the purchase price, and the patient records are the other half. That means the dentist who is buying the practice is paying $500 per patient. And here's one more kicker. Group practices would probably pay even more to acquire that exact practice. What does that tell you?

As you become more remarkable, I encourage you to be realistic about the value of a new patient and invest your promotional dollars accordingly.

INCREASING PRODUCTION

REMARKABLE DENTIST #6

Andrew S. Miller, DDS
Center for Family and Cosmetic Dentistry
Colorado Springs, CO
smilecos.com
facebook.com/smilecos

Year opened: 2006 (practice established 1934)

REMARKABLE NUMBERS:

Annual revenue: $2.8MM (from $300K in 2006)
New patients per month: 90-100
Total Google reviews: 238, as of June 2015
Associates: 1

REMARKABLE TECHNOLOGIES:

CEREC (two of them), digital radiography, intraoral cameras, lasers

REMARKABLE BEHAVIOR:

Dr. Miller was one of the very first dentists to record patient testimonial videos. He started doing them in 2008. (Most of his peers still don't do them.)

Dr. Miller responds appreciatively online to his Google reviews.

When he first took over his practice, he put large, colorful maps on the ceiling. He has since replaced them with TVs, and patients can watch while fully reclined.

Knowing he wouldn't use them if they weren't convenient, Dr. Miller put intraoral cameras in every operatory. He lets the patient see the images on the TV monitor as he takes them, and it has proven to be his most effective case presentation tool

For years, Dr. Miller resisted doing team incentives based on production, in order to prevent the team from pushing dentistry. Once he tried it, he discovered the team became more diligent about billing for all procedures and diagnosed more professionally, without ever recommending more than patients needed.

The practice has heated toilet seats in the rest room.

REMARKABLE QUOTE:

"When it comes to advertising, I'll try anything, but I always go big. It doesn't always work, and I don't expect it to. But in the end, I get mostly great results from doing something bold and unique."

WHAT PEOPLE SAY:

"I have been extremely pleased with everything so far. The day before my first appointment, Dr. Miller called to see if there were any topics he could 'ease my mind about' before my appointment, or if I had any specific questions. I was stunned!"

"Dr. Miller called personally to check on me after I had teeth filled and again when I had my wisdom teeth pulled. How thoughtful! They have a heated toilet, for goodness sake! Customer service is king!"

"I spent 18 years avoiding the dentist due to the horrible experiences I had when I was a child. My wife begged me to go to Andy's dentistry for years and I finally went. Boy was I surprised at how attentive they were to my past experiences. They've tried very hard to help me put those memories behind me."

CHAPTER 43

INNOVATIVE PRODUCTION BOOSTERS

RESPONSIBLE HYGIENE

For 60-something years we've been telling patients they need to come in twice a year. Most of them don't, but even with this attempt on our part, we have 48 percent of people over 30 with some level of periodontal disease, and by 65 that number jumps to 70 percent of the population.[20] In short, we are failing to treat the very significant soft tissue disease that is costing patients their teeth and impairing their immune systems. And we barely go a year before someone discovers some new disease linked to poor oral health. And is that systemic disease caused by caries? No. It's by periodontal disease.

So a truly remarkable practice helps their patients understand that after 35, their dental care is not so much about fighting Mr. Tooth Decay as it is keeping their gums healthy. Which means seeing them more often.

And what happens to a patient when they get their teeth cleaned three times a year? The prophys go much better, there is often no bleeding, and their gums stay pink and healthy. And if they need deep scaling, it needs to be presented in a way that doesn't seem like the practice is just trying to make more money. But when your patients know that everything you do is in their best interest, not yours, then the acceptance rate is much higher.

Which means your patients have healthier gums, nicer breath, will keep their teeth longer, and are not putting extra strain on their immune system. Seems like a worthy effort to me.

From a business standpoint, any practice consultant would tell you that the key to increasing production is tightening your hygiene recall. So take a few minutes and run a report and see what your average recall is on your existing patients, and even limit it to the ones who have been in at least once in the past three years. I think you'll be shocked at the number. Increasing your patients' visits per year elevates their oral health as a priority in their mind. It's just how we behave. The more we neglect ourselves, the longer it slides. I have a theory that if a patient hasn't been in for over a year, they are more likely to slide to two years than they are to come in. I have no hard stats to back it up, but I will get them someday, and I'll bet it's true for a surprising number of people.

Any practice consultant would tell you that the key to increasing production is tightening your hygiene recall.

If you are not able to keep two hygienists busy for every dentist in the practice, then you need to rise to that standard. Something is amiss. Check into the Hygiene Mastery Program in the *Resources* section, or some other practice consultant or coach who can help you make this ratio a reality for your practice. You'll be increasing your production while doing the most important thing of all, taking better care of your patients.

HIGH-PROFIT SERVICES

Ask yourself this: What are you giving your patients that's different from their previous expectation of dentistry? Because you can't just rely on a wonderful team and chairside manner to carry the day. Give them some ammunition, like, "He solved my husband's snoring problem and saved my marriage," or, "I was always afraid of root canals, but my dentist did it herself, and it was nowhere near as bad as I expected. I don't even know what the big deal is."

Here are just a few of the ways you can add high-profit services to your practice:

Sleep apnea appliances. Snoring and apnea affect tens of millions of people, and there are now very effective systems for doing a home study on the patient and then billing the procedure through medical insurance. This solves a big, perhaps life-threatening problem for the patient, and it is entirely within a dentist's capability with a little training. Plus, as I mentioned, it can be billed to the patient's health insurance. Investigate for yourself, but the opportunity is better than it ever has been.

Dermal fillers and BOTOX®. I don't know anyone in health care better with a syringe than a dentist, so who is more qualified to do these types of injections—especially the dermal fillers, which are done intra-orally? More and more states are allowing dentists to do these procedures, and there are excellent courses that can teach you how to do them in a matter of weeks. And if you don't think patients care about this sort of thing, pick up a magazine or two at the checkout line in your local grocery store.

Clear Aligner Therapy. I'm not sure how any general dentist cannot be offering this to patients. Many of your adult patients would be interested in this treatment, if they understood the value of straightening their teeth and the advantages of clear aligners.

Endodontic Therapy. The technology is there to assist general dentists in completing root canal therapy cases to a much greater degree than before. And completing the case yourself has a convenience advantage that the patient will very much appreciate (rather than the three-visit runaround that they get now). This is not to say you should ever undertake a case beyond your comfort zone. That's what endodontists are for.

In addition, lasers allow you to do significantly more periodontal treatment, 3-D imaging broadens your implant capabilities, and cosmetics will continue to be of value to a wide range of patients. And all of these procedures and treatments give your patients a sense of the new style of remarkable dentistry that you offer.

THE FEMALE FACTOR

One of the biggest changes coming to dentistry, and I think one of the best, is the steady increase in the number of female dentists. More than half of the dental students are now female, and this has a few disadvantages—plus some significant added value.

Female dentists are changing the complexion of the dental business. They generally don't have any of the self-esteem issues that some male dentists have because they're not physicians. But statistics have also shown that female dentists are less likely to own practices, and a greater percentage of them will not work full time, at least for part of their careers. These are generalizations, and please don't interpret it to mean that I think women dentists are inferior in any way, or that none of them will own practices or work full time. I've met many who are highly ambitious businesswomen. And very often they do a better job of managing the teams.

My years of experience finding new patients for practices tells me that patients often prefer women over men, just as older people don't like really young doctors and dentists. Some dental consumers have a bias in favor of femininity, assuming a woman dentist will be gentler, have smaller hands, and all sorts of other suppositions. The feminine touch chairside can be very powerful. If you're a woman, great. If not, seriously consider a female associate.

PATIENT FINANCING

How patients will pay for treatment is always a consideration. And very often it will determine the degree of treatment they complete. The problem is, even though most practices offer financing, they don't present it or they don't mention it at the right time or in the right way.

I recently heard from Bete Johnson, Vice President of Business Development at CareCredit, that more than 80 percent of the patients who finance their dentistry through them *pay no interest*. That means they pay off the loan not just on time, but in a short enough period where no interest accrues. Does this not tell you that most people just need a little time—that they simply don't have the money right now? To me it also means that you are doing them a disservice by not offering financing options, because we all know that postponing treatment is almost never in the patient's best interest.

A study also revealed that if CareCredit were not available, almost half of patients would have postponed the treatment or only done a part of the treatment. This is especially true for people under 35. Half is a lot in terms of impact on your production!

A remarkable practice lets patients know about financing options. They are comfortable talking about it and offering it, and they make it as easy as possible for the patient to apply. CareCredit can train your team on the best way to present financing. They know what works based on working with thousands of dentists and can vastly improve your results. I mention them because they are the largest and have the most extensive training, and also because 80 percent of practices use CareCredit, so I'm just trying to get you to take advantage of a free resource.

You may say, "Well, they deny a lot of people." They deny people who don't have good credit. So what—you want to finance those people yourself? If they don't have a good payment history, why would you want to get in that line?

If you're looking for new patients, please understand that one of the first considerations is if you offer financing. Which is why you MUST have a link on your website where patients can apply for credit for treatment. You want patients to be able to do this before their appointment and get an instant credit decision. CareCredit can do this for you and can even add their Payment Calculator to your site.

If you're looking for new patients, understand that one of their first considerations is if you offer financing.

You see why I like them? They get marketing to patients and provide tremendous resources. Maybe you want to have another financing resource as well, and that's up to you, but in my mind offering CareCredit is essential.

INTERNAL DENTAL PLANS

Along the same lines as financing are internal dental plans. Since, in my opinion, many practices are essentially under attack by the dental insurance companies, it is good to have viable alternatives for patients. The advantage is that you control it, essentially eliminating the middle man. (The salary for the CEO of Washington Dental Services in 2010 was $1.3 million, before bonus, and the top executives took out a total of $5.8 million. That's some middle man under the guise of a nonprofit organization.) And it's your own practice plan, so it keeps the patient within your practice.

The program I'm most familiar with is Plan for Health, so I'll describe that one.

Plan for Health is a complete "in-house" dental membership program you can offer your patients. Obviously, this will help fill the schedule and increase your cash flow. And it also compensates for the growing desire on the consumer side for some sort of dental coverage when their employer doesn't offer any. Also, you get to set the pricing and the amount of discount you offer on procedures.

The plan allows patients to prepay and preschedule their whole year of preventive treatment. It offers three types of memberships (Child, Adult, and Perio). The membership fee can be charged annually or monthly, and includes three dental hygiene visits for adults (two for children, four for perio patients), digital X-rays, exams, and a discount on procedures and products.

This type of plan is ideal for cash patients who are not on an existing insurance plan, as it is much more cost-effective than an independent dental plan through an outside insurance company. And it also works for patients as a supplement to their existing dental coverage because it is more comprehensive.

By enrolling your practice in Plan for Health, you receive full support and training. This includes an initial supply of brochures, a training manual, three one-hour interactive web-based/conference call trainings, membership agreements for the patients, marketing materials, and templates and pricing recommendations. Plan for Health incorporates right into your practice management software. They train your team on how to set up the plan properly for health codes and accounting procedures. You can promote this plan on your website as well as to your existing patients.

With Plan for Health's program, you set the pricing and the discount levels yourself, and the company is not attached to your production revenue, unlike some other plans. Best of all, it's designed to get your patients in three times a year, and this fulfills the hygiene strategy that I talked about earlier.

A word of warning: Do not try to craft one of these plans on your own, or you will end up violating some state regulations. Plan for Health has vetted its program in all 50 states.

A similar internal program is offered by Quality Dental Plan. I would seriously consider one of these as part of being remarkably affordable and accommodating to your patients.

CHAPTER 44

DEMAND-BASED PRICING

What exactly is demand-based pricing? It is essentially variations in the price offered to consumers relative to the desirability of a specific day or time, or speed of delivery. For example, rental car companies charge more on weekends. Electronic toll roads charge more during rush hours. Hotels charge more around holidays. Faster shipping costs more. Last-minute airline tickets are much more expensive than buying a month in advance. Movie matinees are cheaper. It's simply price-flexing based on demand or lack thereof.

This pricing principle could easily be applied to dental practices. It ties in with becoming more convenient.

For example, if you're finding that the evenings and early mornings are booking out months in advance, maybe you should increase the fee for a prophy at those times and perhaps lower it for other times. Basic economics is to see what pricing the traffic will bear. When I've suggested this, a few office managers asked what to do when the appointment is paid for by dental coverage. I have two solutions. One is to charge a separate reservation fee for those times of the week. This could be for any procedure. It is simply explained as limited availability.

The second choice is to only allow fee-for-service patients to book those times. You can always waive these rules or fees for VIP patients, like airlines do with platinum frequent fliers. Patients who've been with you over five years, or had full mouth restorations, or never missed an appointment can all get special treatment.

Demand-based pricing also includes *when* the payment is charged, as well as how much. Hotels charge for holiday periods in advance—usually nonrefundable, too—and restaurants will demand a credit card for holidays or some weekends, and they charge your card regardless of whether or not you show up. You could, too.

Occasionally I meet dentists who say, "I've tried Saturday hours, but I get a lot of no-shows, even with long-time patients."

As I mentioned earlier, my suggestion to them is to tell patients, "If you want to book Saturday, that day is in high demand, so we require prepayment of the appointment." People tend to show up much more if they have prepaid, especially if they are going to lose the money. (You can always waive that if it's a good patient or a valid reason.) And if they don't want to pay it, then they don't take the valuable time slot and instead schedule themselves into your regular workday, where a no-show hurts less.

Many dentists using CEREC charge more for those restorations, even though it takes them less time overall. Why? Because it's more convenient to the patient.

Someone needs something done in a hurry? Rush orders always have a surcharge. They need veneers or implants, and they need a rapid turnaround for an event? Then they get the rush charge. If they want the dentistry in a hurry from a remarkable dentist, they should be willing to pay for you to work on a Sunday or pay the rush charge to your lab and pay your team members' overtime. It's pure profit after the overtime. And there is nothing unethical or unprofessional about it. That type of limiting belief gets you nowhere and is simply a pointless story you've told yourself because you're afraid to ask for the money you deserve.

On the other end of the pricing spectrum, you can also charge less for weaker time slots when you are in the office. This lets people know that you are willing to accommodate them if pricing is an issue. Slow hours, slow weeks, or last-minute appointments can all have a reduced fee. Be careful, because these time slots might suddenly fill up really quickly. What would that tell you? Price is an issue for your patient base, and you need to find more ways—like financing or an internal plan—to deal with that.

There should always be an after-hours emergency surcharge (paid by credit card over the phone or with cash before you start treatment), which can be waived at your discretion.

Will this type of pricing turn some people off? Maybe. But it's not the first place they've experienced it. Generation Y is so used to it that they hardly notice. Convenience costs more almost everywhere. But each dentist has only 35 hours a week to deliver dentistry, so why not make the most of those hours and make sure someone is in a chair as often as possible, paying as much as possible? And if you are going outside of your normal hours, it's perfectly reasonable to charge more.

Also, if you read my first book, one of the concepts I mention is how and what you charge affects the perception of value. Consumers think this way about everything, and when you have demand-based pricing, it communicates that your services have a greater value. This is a beautiful marketing message: You are perceived as a better practitioner clinically because you can charge this way.

Demand-based pricing communicates that your services have a greater value.

Note: Sometimes team members resist working those hours, but if you have demand-based pricing, you can pay them extra per hour for those time slots. It's not hard to make these calculations to ensure that there is more profit in it for everyone going the extra mile.

You may ask, "But doesn't this fly in the face of being more affordable?" I don't think so, because affordable is always relative to convenience and availability. Southwest Airlines may be the cheapest airline, but try buying a ticket the day before you want to fly. This approach could also allow you to be more affordable to patients who need it and are willing to compromise on convenience. You can flex in both directions, just as the airlines do.

Will these ideas work in every practice everywhere in the country? Of course not. But some of them may be just right for you. Of course, always comply with what's legal in your state. (But there usually is a way.)

CHAPTER 45

WANT TO WIN?
GET A GOOD COACH

Living in Los Angeles, I meet more than my share of actors. Not just the famous ones, but the ones trying to make it. Many of them are at the "undiscovered" stage of their careers— and they're pure artists. By that I mean they *love* acting. They are passionate about the process of creating a character and performing. And some of them are extremely talented, but are starving, because they have not adjusted to the idea that they are working in an industry trying to make a profit, not just art.

Tom Cruise, on the other hand, knows that he is in a business. He loves acting and works as hard—or harder—than almost anyone in the industry on his performances. He has been the lead in more than 30 films, has won three Golden Globes®, and has been nominated for three Oscars®. But he is also ranked #3 in all-time box office revenue ($6.5 billion so far) because he understands the *business* of acting, perhaps better than almost anyone.

So what does that have to do with dentistry? In my experience, the best dentists clinically are artist/engineer personalities. They want to do great dentistry and train themselves constantly to get better. But many of them are in practices that are struggling financially. Despite being extraordinary "artists," their careers are not paying off. Just like the "pure" actors, they don't like the idea of promoting themselves or focusing on the business aspects of their practice, and they don't feel the need to understand their "audience."

Tom Cruise has a PR team, an acting coach, a manager, an agent, a financial advisor, and business partners in his production company. Why? Because to succeed in acting, you need all of those things, in addition to talent.

The successful dentists I know all have their outside team as well. They use a practice consultant to coach them, work with a financial advisor as well as a CPA, use outside marketing resources, and have a trusted relationship with their distributor representative. And they make sure that their office managers are constantly updating their business skills and that their team is always learning, growing, and adapting.

You might say, "But all that is expensive!" But you know what else is expensive? Houses. Cars. Kids' educations. Travel. Retirement. That's why you need to be financially successful as a dentist, not just clinically excellent. That takes investment. Tom Cruise pays his manager 10 percent of his income because he *earns it!* His acting coach isn't an expense, he's an investment in growth. His financial advisor doesn't cost him money, he makes him money. And all of these people do these things so that Tom can focus on his performance.

Of course, that doesn't mean he doesn't understand the business aspects of his career. You can bet he's paying close attention to it. (Just as you should.)

There are also some actors who start to achieve success and believe they did it themselves, based entirely on their talent. So they fire their manager and agent, or leave their successful sitcom so they can pursue a movie career, despite their agent's advice on the self-destructive aspects of the timing. And their career goes into a 20-year lull.

Dentists do this too, with coaches and consultants. They bring in a coach and start growing two or three years in a row at 20 percent and then convince themselves it was all their doing, not the coach's efforts. So they fire the coach. And two years later, they're right back to producing what they did four years ago. If Tom Cruise fires his agent, it's because he found a better one, not because he thinks he can do it all on his own. Don't make this classic mistake. None of us achieve the highest levels of success without coaching. We all have blind spots. We have personal biases and limiting beliefs. We're human, not computers, and none of us is so brilliant that we can invent or improve every aspect of a business without guidance.

> I do not know any successful person who has not only had one coach, but a series of mentors throughout their career.

One of the most basic principles of success is the willingness to be coached. I do not know any successful businessperson, including myself, who has not only had one coach, but a series of mentors throughout their career. It is the fastest way to the next level of accomplishment, because other people can often easily observe what we are completely oblivious to.

Long-term success in dentistry is not an impossible mission, but a noble one. You're helping people, and the only way you can keep doing it in the next 20 years is by running your business extremely well. That takes a team, a coach, and business discipline. Run reports, set daily production goals. Know your metrics and compare them to your peers. A coach can tell you how you measure up to the standard.

Bernie Stoltz, the CEO of Fortune Management, the largest practice-coaching business in healthcare, preaches a philosophy from Tony Robbins of constant and never-ending improvement—C.A.N.I. It is rooted in a lifetime of Tony's personal experiences, where he has seen that no matter where someone is, they need to make a conscious effort to get to the next level of success and to keep their business thriving.

We also forget to do what we already know. The reason famed UCLA basketball coach John Wooden spent 90 percent of his time reminding his players of the fundamentals is because he knew that we all drift away. We are in a constant battle with our own human nature. If you play golf, how often do your old habits come back? Usually they've been back for a while before someone else points them out to you.

Every successful athlete has at least one coach, simply because they don't know what they're doing wrong and how they can get better. A good consultant can get you and your team there faster. You can lay out your vision—your road to remarkable—and a good consultant or practice coach will help you realize that dream without hitting every pothole along the way.

CHAPTER 46

THE GREATEST
CONFIDENCE
BUILDER

M y personal dentist gets a staggering amount of continuing education every year (over 300 hours). I consider
him one of the most skilled and best-trained dentists in the
country. I get to benefit from this skill, but I also noticed another result of this much training. He is tremendously confident in his abilities—and it shows in his case presentation and
results in much higher case acceptance.

The remarkable dentists that I've highlighted in this book are
all CE addicts. Their desire to get better is almost insatiable.
And this is true of many of the dentists that I've interacted
with over the years. I have been fortunate to spend a good
deal of time at Spear Education in Scottsdale, Arizona, which
offers a wide variety of courses, particularly in the integration
of technology into your practice, and the refinement of skills in
implants and single-visit dentistry.

Dr. Frank Spear is a gifted speaker and I believe an extraordinary clinician. But the dimensions of the center go far beyond what he personally has to offer. There are dozens of teachers, trainers, and mentors of remarkable capability, some of whom I number among my good friends. And it has shown me that whatever level you are at clinically, there is always more. And with the rapid advancement of CEREC and GALILEOS technology, for example, learning how those devices work together elevates the dentistry you can offer to an amazing level.

However, embedded in this clinical training environment is all the wisdom of Imtiaz Manji, a man who has trained dentists for decades to not only run great practices, but to be great leaders. He has created an environment of personal growth and mutual support among the dentists who regularly visit there that I personally consider unparalleled.

I'm certain there are other dental training centers of a high caliber all around the country. My point in describing Spear is for you to find one that makes you the dentist you most want to become, and even discover the dentist you never imagined you could become.

Here is an observation about success that I learned from my interactions with entrepreneurs: You are the average of the five people you spend the most time with. This might give you pause and cause for reflection. But in looking back on my decades of experience in business, I have come to believe this more and more. I try to spend as much time as possible with people who are wiser, more spiritual, and more experienced that I am. And it has enriched me immeasurably. And

I certainly did not always do this. But once I started, there was no turning back.

A good friend, Gary Takacs, who runs Takacs Learning Center, is one of those people. Not only is he perhaps the most positive person I've ever met, he has decades of experience working with dental practices and gives me constant insight into the day-to-day challenges of running a dental business. I recommend you find a Gary or two yourself.

Fortune Management has a group of dental clients called the Platinum Circle. These are top performers who get together at least twice a year and share everything that is working for them in every aspect of their lives and practices. Invariably, they inspire one another to new levels of what is possible, and each member comes from a place of generosity and abundance. Just as I've seen at Spear, this is a phenomenal gift they give to one another.

If you are a team member, this same principle of self-challenge applies. The more you improve yourself, the more confident you will be in communication with patients. If you're an office manager, the American Association of Dental Office Managers is an exceptional and unique peer organization. Whatever your role in the practice, there are groups, meetings, and study clubs that can up your game and make your career a whole lot more interesting at the same time.

Ask yourself whether some of your peers are more successful than you, happier than you, more ambitious than you, more spiritual than you? Make sure that some of them are exactly that. I'm not suggesting you abandon your current peers, but I am strongly recommending that you move out of your comfort zone and boost your average.

And I'm not just talking about people with more stuff than you. I think that's a pointless measurement. It's about genuinely successful people who are striving and learning and growing all the time. Surround yourself with these kinds of people, occasionally immerse yourself in a whole group of them, and you will feel the pull to new levels of personal and professional fulfillment. And at the same time, as you work to improve yourself, you'll be improving the average for your peers. It's a virtuous cycle.

Here's another great idea: Go to other dentists' offices. You have to see a dentist at least every six months, right? Don't let your own team always do your prophys. (Although they should sometimes so you know how good they are!). You and your team members should all go to get treated by other dentists and hygienists. Have an exchange program with your friends.

Or you can take it to the next level and actively mentor other dentists, particularly younger dentists, who are going to be struggling with new technology and a much higher degree of debt, on average. They will need your guidance. And don't expect anything in return, and it will be even more satisfying to see that you've reached into another dentist's life and made a difference, just as you do with your patients. When it comes to being generous, don't just share your wealth—share your wealth of knowledge.

This is all part of a philosophy of abundance, which is what I want to talk about in the next section.

SECTION EIGHT:

THE UPWARD
SPIRAL

CHAPTER 47

SCARCITY
VERSUS
ABUNDANCE

This last section is about embracing and achieving change. I'm sure that if you've read this far, or have had occasion to see me speak, you get the sense that I like to challenge people's mindsets and get them to move into what I call their discomfort zone. I do this because I've learned that all real change starts with a change of mindset.

Now, if you ask people what's held them back in life, they'll have all kinds of excuses that they will label as causes. They will say it's the economy, or their teachers, or their parents, or their ethnicity that's limited them. Otherwise they'll blame society, their gender, their height, or the government. When in actuality, what holds most people back are their own beliefs. Tony Robbins calls these "limiting beliefs," which I've learned is extremely accurate. And one of the most limiting beliefs of all is one of scarcity.

This is how the scarcity belief translates into people's lives. They believe there isn't enough opportunity. There isn't enough money to go around. There isn't enough love in the world. So for someone to win, someone else has to lose. The problem with a limiting belief is that once you believe it, it becomes true for you. It creates this world around you, full of limitations and negativity and resentment. The other choice—and make no mistake, it is a choice—is to believe in abundance. This is what Tony calls an empowering belief.

I see far too many dentists fall into this trap of scarcity. It's almost like they teach it in dental school. I hear it all the time. "There aren't enough patients." "The economy is bad." "I can't get good employees." The problem is, saying it doesn't make it true, it just makes it true for *them*. There are thousands of dentists who believe there are tons of opportunity, and that they make their own economy, and have an amazing team.

We live in the most abundant industry, in the most abundant time in history, in the most abundant country in the world.

So why believe in abundance? We live in the most abundant time in history, in the most abundant country in the world, in one of the most abundant industries. In fact, dentistry has been evaluated by a government study as the most profitable industry in America.[21] Now you think, "Hey, that's not my experience," but it *can* be once you escape gravity. And the first stage of that rocket is this mindset of abundance.

The abundance mindset launches a cycle that expands as you build a culture and a team based on it. Then, as you begin to incorporate new technology, you become faster and better. Now you can attract exceptional team members because, frankly, your practice is a blast to work in. And you have money to give them bonuses and incentives. You can then invest in a more inviting practice design. Production increases and profit really increases. So now you can promote your practice more, and you can get more training and add more technology. You can bring on an associate and increase your treatment hours, becoming more convenient. You may even reach a point of adding a specialist or two. You can be more profitable and more affordable at the same time. And it all goes spiraling upward.

Conversely, if you choose to believe in scarcity, you won't risk anything. You won't do anything to become even slightly remarkable. You will try to save money on supplies. Cheaper burs and cheaper labs, and lower pay for team members, which increases turnover. New technology is out of reach and so is remodeling. You attempt advertising, but few patients stay long-term or accept treatment. Instead of the upward spiral allowing you to become more affordable, you have to literally become the cheapest dentist in order to attract patients. And the word will spread online. And the downward spiral will continue.

Another thought on abundance: At the core of abundance is a spirit of generosity. When it comes to this, those of you who work in dentistry are lucky. You don't have to donate money to charity, although many of you do. Just donating your skills can have powerful positive repercussions in someone's life.

We all know that there are many people in our communities who cannot afford even basic dental care. Helping get a child out of pain so that they can concentrate and not fall behind in school is an amazing gift to be able to give. Making it possible for that single mother to keep her smile when every penny she makes goes to keeping a roof over her kids' heads is an act of generosity infinitely more satisfying than some charity dinner. You have the ability to change the course of someone's life in just an hour or two. That's a powerful gift. Give of it generously. The dentists I know who do one day a month of charitable dentistry say it is their favorite day of the month, and the most gratifying. Don't cheat yourself out of this experience.

With a mindset of abundance, you are ready to bring change into your practice behavior. But getting people to change is difficult (especially changing ourselves!) and it's even more challenging to make it last. So let's get practical and talk about how to get it done.

CHAPTER 48

THE ULTIMATE
CHANGE STRATEGY

"Not making a decision is a decision." Tim Ferriss

So you've decided to bring change to your practice and become remarkable. How will you make it happen?

In my travels, studies, and encounters with highly successful people, I've discovered what I think is the most successful pathway to bring about permanent changes in myself and my business. And I know it will work for you and your practice.

There are two different methods to apply, depending on whether you're changing a situation or changing behavior.

METHOD ONE:

If it is a situation that you believe needs to be changed, then it comes down to the Nike method: *Just do it.* If there is a thing that needs to be done, just get to it as soon as possible. Hesitation and overthinking only delay the inevitable need to act. If you need to fire someone, fire them tomorrow. Don't wait, don't agonize, don't second-guess yourself. Do it. This applies to many things. Changing software. Moving offices. Hiring a coach. Buying technology. Adding an insurance plan. There is no way to make the perfect decision. Good leaders know that it's about making the best decision you can and taking action—and then making that decision work for you.

I can guarantee that you will not always make the right decision. No one does. But inaction has become riskier and riskier, and the only way to activate the upward spiral is to be willing to take those risks, knowing you won't always be right.

METHOD TWO:

Now let's talk about how you create changes in behavior or ability. This is something I learned from the author Tim Ferriss. It is based on a story of a PhD student who had made a promise to himself that he was going to write *at least one sentence* of his thesis every single day, no matter what. It didn't matter if it was three in the morning and he came home half drunk, he was going to sit at that computer and knock out at least one line.

The result was he finished his thesis before everyone else in his class. Why? Because he tricked himself. Changing yourself is very often a trick, because the trick is getting started. As it turned out, he didn't always write just one sentence. Sometimes he wrote two. And other times he wrote a page and sometimes he rewrote three pages. But he started—and he also let himself off the hook—with the first sentence. I'll talk about why this whole formula is critical when I break down the process.

Here are the three steps to creating change:

1. Decide to do something different.
2. Work on it every day.
3. Make the daily goal embarrassingly small.

STEP ONE: DECIDE

You must decide what you want to change and what that change will entail. Sometimes you will be doing something *differently*—that is, not the same way you have been doing it. And other times you will need to do something *different,* meaning an entirely new approach. But all change starts with an acceptance that doing nothing—or doing something the way you've been doing it—is no longer working.

There is another element to this. We often reach a point where we are doing something and we want better results, so we work harder at doing the same thing. This will reach a point of diminishing returns, and we need to find a different way. The different choice yields a whole new level of results, once we learn to do it well. (Remember the principle of slowing down to speed up.) The answer very often isn't to *do something harder*, but *do something else*.

The answer very often isn't to do something harder, but do something else.

It may be that you've decided to do something personally, like lose weight or start a retirement plan. You will still need to find a different way to get your result, as you've likely tried before and failed. For professional changes, this may take some research or some coaching to come up with the change strategy.

For example, you could decide that your practice is ready for single-visit dentistry. You must buy the technology, of course, but then you have to commit to integrating it into your practice.

So commit to the decision, and then follow the next steps.

STEP TWO: DAILY ACTION

Commit to do some action as part of the change on a daily basis. This is more powerful than you may think. It's not just that it gradually aggregates to a larger result. It does something to your brain. It redefines you to yourself. When you do something every day, it starts to become part of who you are, rather than just something you're doing. It creates this continuum that translates into "I am this kind of person."

For example, I write every single day. I could write occasionally, or in bursts here and there throughout the year, and still consider myself a writer. But when I do it every day, my *brain* believes I'm a writer. And I become a better writer faster. And I write more.

In your case, staying with the CEREC example, doing a restoration every day will have a much greater impact on your progress than doing several all in one day a week. You will begin a progression that builds on itself and gets you further faster.

And this applies to anything you want to change. You want to get good at asking for referrals? Ask someone every day. You want to learn a musical instrument or a language? Work on it every day. You want to save for retirement? Spend a little less every day, and stash the money in a 401(k) or an IRA.

Daily is the key. Being a weekend warrior is never really going to get you into shape compared to daily exercise. If you study Spanish one day a week, you'll forget half of what you learned by the time you get back to it.

You may need a resource to improve the skill or to guide you through the steps of the change. It could be training, or coaching, or online videos. That all depends on what you've decided to change.

STEP THREE: SMALL GOALS

This is really the big one. Make the daily goal embarrassingly small. This is our big mistake when we decide we want to change or improve something. We often have the big goal, whether it's to become fluent in Spanish, or learn to do complex implant cases, or lose 40 pounds. But what we end up doing is making the steps to the goal too large, and so we stumble a few times and eventually drift back to doing nothing.

I know I'm always harping on human nature. But going against it is almost always a fool's errand. We need to trick ourselves. Who cares why? It works.

Do you really want to get in shape? Do some simple exercise every day. You could join a gym and promise that you're going three times a week and working out for an hour, but what happens? You miss a day because you left work late and you're too tired now. Or you don't have time to work out and take a shower after, so you skip it. Instead, you could say, "I'm going to do at least 20 pushups every day." That's it. But do it every single day, and you know what will happen? After a month, you're going to really feel it. And 20 pushups will have turned into 50.

You'll also do longer workouts sometimes. I can't tell you how many workouts I've started where I just didn't feel like it, so I said, "I'm just going to do the first exercise." And I do it—and then I do one more. And 45 minutes later, I'm sweating and feeling great. But other times I just do the first exercise. But either way, my brain believes I'm someone who exercises and reinforces the behavior and provides the motivation. I've redefined myself to myself.

The only way you will successfully work on your goal every day is if it's ridiculous not to. One sentence of the PhD, remember? One CEREC restoration a day. Ask for one referral a day. Eat one bite less of every meal. Save $5 a day.

I've read that you'll progress faster with 10 minutes of practice a day on a musical instrument than if you did an hour twice a week. I've also learned that you can hold a conversation in almost any language if you just learn 2,500 words. Do two words a day and in three years you're there. How long would two words take? Two minutes? And once you start speaking, won't it go faster and faster? Of course it will.

What if it's something you can't work on every day, like doing implants? Then do something toward getting better at it. Watch a video a day. Practice what you've learned however you can. Study a different 3-D image every day to see how you would evaluate the case. It's always possible to find that bite-sized step toward your goal. You could even vary those things, as long as you do *something*. It doesn't have to be the same exact thing every day.

The other powerful aspect of the small daily step goal is that you don't tip over. We've all exercised so hard that we couldn't move for the next three days. That defeats the purpose here. If you're learning to use CEREC, don't start by restoring a whole quadrant in the first week. You'll fail for sure and park the device for the next year. You want to gradually increase your ability, so that you can always come back to it every single day.

Let's say your goal is to be comfortable presenting cases over $10,000, and currently you go into flop sweats as soon as the case is more than $3,000. Don't try to present an $8,000 case tomorrow. Do $3,500 until it seems easy, then bump it up again. You work in health care, so you understand dosage tolerance—apply it!

I also recommend doing your step goal as early in the day as possible, because you know what happens? You do it once, it was pretty easy, and you find yourself doing it once more. Just as you might expand the time that you work on it once you've tricked yourself, accomplishing it early in the day creates an urge to have another little success. And suddenly, you'll have your PhD.

EXTRA MAGIC

If you really want to get to your goal, there is one more element that you can add that plays right into human nature (of course!). That is to declare your goal publicly. This solidifies the commitment to do something different. And it elicits support from your friends, peers, and team members.

So as the dentist, you would say to one of your peers, "I'm going to fully integrate CEREC into my practice within the next 24 months. And I'm going to do at least one restoration every day." Do you see that you've included both aspects of the change—the overall goal and the daily step goal?

Or a team member might commit to her goal by saying, "I'm going to be the top source of new referrals in the office by asking at least one patient a day to recommend us."

This process works for almost anything. Whatever your dreams are, take a bite a day.

PICK ONE THING

I want to reiterate a point I made earlier in this book: Don't try to change five behavioral things at once. Change them in sequence in order of importance, and make sure that each change is integrated into your practice behavior before you start the next one. Social science says this takes an average of six weeks, flexing a week or two in either direction depending on how difficult the change is.

When you feel that you have gotten a rhythm to the first change, that your everyday actions are part of your routine, then add the next change. This goes for the practice as well as the team members individually. And it refers only to Method Two. With Method One, you are taking action, so you're not integrating a behavior. You can knock those out one by one in fairly rapid succession.

Remember the question I posed in Chapter 11: *What is the one thing I can be doing right now that would make everything else easier or not necessary?*

I love this question, and I use it all the time. I use it on a large scale by asking the question about our business as a whole, and then we bring it down to department levels, and then individuals, and then daily activities. In fact, it's how I finished this book, because I didn't let lesser priorities interrupt my writing. You can apply it in your office activities, and the answer might be: "Always answer the phone, and do it with skill, purpose, and a smile." That would certainly make a lot of things easier or not necessary, wouldn't it?

And at an even higher level, as I said earlier, building trust with your patients makes everything easier. But you need to add all the elements that make that happen. Throughout this book I've given you many different changes you could implement on your road to remarkable. Use this question to prioritize them, and the results will show quickly.

CHAPTER 49

WHAT WILL PEOPLE
SAY ABOUT YOU?

I've tried to lay out a positive vision of the future of dentistry and the wonderful opportunities for your practice in the years ahead. And though it may seem edgy and out of reach, I believe that aspiring to the three-part goal of providing higher quality dentistry, in less time, and more affordably is not only possible, but the surest way to guarantee your long-term success.

In the end, what you make of your practice as the dentist and what you bring to it as a team member are entirely up to you. But what people think of you, and what they share with the world about you, is entirely up to them. I hope they say things like this (all excerpted from real reviews, by the way):

"He explained everything so well."

"I've never felt so cared for in a dental visit."

"She changed my life."

"The dentist was so compassionate."

"Everyone in the office was so sweet and happy."

"I finally found a dentist who really listens to me."

"I never knew a dental visit could be like this."

"The doctor is knowledgeable, confident, and patient."

"I have already recommended them to all my friends."

"I feel lucky to have found them."

"For this level of care they're totally affordable."

"They are all so fun to be around."

"Thanks to them, I finally understand how important my teeth are."

"You can see the passion they all have for dentistry."

"I love my dentist; he's remarkable."

"I can't imagine going to anyone else. She's remarkable."

Much of what I've presented in this book should be treated as a starting point, a leap into new ways of viewing your business, your practice, your team, and your patients. My hope is I've given you some of the tools and insights to move you faster and deeper in the direction of your dreams. I wish you a rich and satisfying career, and a joyful and generous life, filled with appreciative patients, loving friends, and close family.

ACKNOWLEDGMENTS

As always, a book doesn't write itself, and an author doesn't get it all done on his own. This is especially true in my case. My list of supporters, mentors, and friends in the industry is long and getting longer, and each in some way contributed to making this book better.

It starts with my remarkable team at 1-800-DENTIST. As a whole, I couldn't be prouder of our company culture and the dedication everyone has to do their best day after day. They provide feedback and research that has inspired much of what is in this book.

My heartfelt thanks to Betsy Roddy, our marketing director, who kept me on track and undistracted throughout the whole process, and gave the manuscript that all-important final read.

To Brian Becker, my editor-in-chief, who we brought in from "retirement" to mastermind the revisions of the book. He knows my voice, my quirks, and my previous book and blogs like few others. I couldn't have done it without him. My deepest thanks.

A big thanks and hug to Kim Fuller, who shepherds me through my travels and lectures, and manages the flow of all information regarding the book and everything else that is necessary to keep me sane and focused. And thanks also to Tom Owens, who never fails to spark a better turn of phrase, or point out a clumsy one. I respect your mind and value your judgment.

Now for the industry folks.

To Jeff Slovin and Michael Augins at Sirona Dental Systems, my deepest thanks for the inspiration, support—and most of all—friendship. Your company is one to be proud of, and that is always a result of great leadership. I look forward to many years of adventure together.

Huge thanks to Paul Guggenheim and Scott Anderson at Patterson Dental for your continued support and friendship. Your culture inspires me, as does your integrity and positive spirit. And truly the thanks extends to all your marvelous branch managers, territory representatives, and support people. They make working in this industry a daily joy for me.

To Dr. Howard Farran. You are and have always been one of my greatest supporters, and make me believe in myself. Your lectures never fail to inform and astound me, and I treasure the long years of friendship.

A great big thanks goes to Gary Takacs. We go back to the beginning together, and it seems like it's just been one long, gratifying, and inspiring conversation. You're a great friend, and a gift to this industry.

To Ron Joyal, who has been instrumental in the creation of a corporate culture of integrity and trust and caring, and who inspires me every day. You're a man who never stops learning and growing. And no one could ask for a finer brother.

To Bernie Stoltz—thanks for tracking me down that fateful day so long ago. Our relationship has given me so many gifts, both personal and professional, that I don't think I'd be where I am without you. Or at least, it would have been a lot less fun getting here.

Thanks especially to Jennifer Chevalier at Fortune Management. You are the "invisible hand" that keeps Fortune running, and I'm grateful for your support, your insights, and especially your friendship.

And to all the Fortune Management team across the country, you come from the very best place—a desire to make a difference. And the determination to do it the right way every day.

To my dear, dear friend Imtiaz Manji. I perhaps owe you the greatest thanks. You are the truest definition of a friend—selfless in everything you do for me, brutally candid when you need to be, supportive, inspiring, caring. I treasure your friendship beyond measure.

And a special thanks to my dear friends Kaleim and Rezwan Manji, who have grown to be business powerhouses in their own right. From the days of Young & Motivated, I've been able to share in your amazing journey, and sincerely believe it is only the beginning.

To everyone in the publishing and seminar side of the industry, I want to express my deep gratitude. You do a great job, and it is an honor to work alongside you as we help practices grow and succeed.

And to all my blog followers, thanks for reading, commenting, and sharing.

To my Remarkable Dentists (I'm claiming them as my own), Andy, Nhi, Paul, Craig, Brian, and Kirsten: Your stories inspire me and demonstrate that what I present in this book is not theory but proven every day by you in your practices. My deepest thanks for your openness and sharing.

And to all the other remarkable dentists that I've met out on the road. I learn from each and every one of you, and from all your team members as well. It's an honor and a privilege to work with you.

And lastly, to everyone working every day in this remarkable industry of ours: Your work is noble, and I'm grateful to be able to serve you as you help people in spite of themselves.

RESOURCES AND RECOMMENDED READING

These are various books, businesses, services, and individuals in the dental industry that I find very helpful. I consider them trusted resources for growing your practice, training your employees, protecting your business, and creating a better work environment and more satisfying life. And I don't get a kickback from any one of them.

BOOKS:

Start with Why and *Leaders Eat Last* by Simon Sinek
> These two books, read in sequence, will help you find your true purpose and understand what true leadership entails, and guide you toward molding yourself into the best you can be.

Good to Great by Jim Collins

I've never met a business owner who couldn't benefit from this book. I consider it the best business book ever written. Follow it up with *Great by Choice* and you'll be way ahead of the game.

MONEY: Master the Game: 7 Simple Steps to Financial Freedom by Tony Robbins

For the dentist and the team, there is no more comprehensive book on avoiding the many pitfalls of saving, investing, and managing your money, while learning the most advantageous ways to preserve and grow your practice. This is also where you can strategize the best retirement plan for your team and combine it with your incentive program.

The One Thing: The Surprisingly Simple Truth Behind Extraordinary Results by Gary Keller

The best book on defining your priorities and executing them.

Hire to Inspire by Jennifer Chevalier and Yolanda Mangrum, DDS

This is a marvelous compendium of insights and practical steps to exceptional team-building from the best business minds in dentistry.

It All Starts with Marketing: 201 Marketing Tips for Growing a Dental Practice by Anne Marie Gorczyca, DMD

This is an excellent complement to my first book, and is full of practical tips that any practice can apply.

Dynamic Dentistry by Linda Miles

Powerful, practical advice from one of the masters. Her understanding of patients and the most effective ways to communicate with them are the foundation for a great practice. www.asklindamiles.com

Switch: How to Change Things When Change is Hard by Chip and Dan Heath

This is a phenomenal book, often counter-intuitive, on the most effective ways to bring about change in your life, your practice, and your team.

Predictably Irrational by Dan Ariely

Most of my insights on human nature and the bizarreness of decision-making either come from listening to patients or reading this book.

Making It Easy for Patients to Say "Yes" by Dr. Paul Homoly, CSP

In my experience, this is one of the best approaches out there to improve your case presentation—available as a book or audio program. www.paulhomoly.com

Great Communication = Great Success and *Collect What You Produce* by Dr. Cathy Jameson

Both are cornerstone books on practice management. Not to be missed. www.jamesonmanagement.com

How to Build the Dental Practice of Your Dreams (Without Killing Yourself) by David Moffet

A finely tuned, step-by-step approach to creating a great dental experience, from an Australian's perspective.

PRACTICE MANAGEMENT AND TEAM COACHING:

Fortune Management—they are the only practice management company with individual franchises around the country, so your consultant actually lives in your city. They are the health care licensee for all of Anthony Robbin's life-coaching material, and I have never seen a practice that didn't grow 20 percent in the first year working with them. Also, three of the six Remarkable Dentists featured in this book are Fortune clients. www.fortunemgmt.com

HUMAN RESOURCES:

HR for Health has a comprehensive service that will keep you in compliance and solve a lot of your day-to-day headaches and challenges being a small business. Cloud based, it deals with every aspect of employee management, including payroll. www.hrforhealth.com

JOB SEARCH AND POSTING:

DentalPost has over 600,000 dental professional users and over 34,000 dentists/offices posting jobs, making it the best marketplace to find new team members. It also includes employee personality profiling tools. www.dentalpost.net

TEAM TRAINING AND COACHING:

Gary Takacs and his *Takacs Learning Center* is a comprehensive and very personal coaching service. It includes *The Thriving Dentist,* which are podcasts interviewing the top experts in the industry. He is also partners with Remarkable Dentist Dr. Paul Neilson in Phoenix. www.takacslearningcenter.com

SOCIAL MEDIA OUTSOURCING:

You will always have your own responsibilities with social media, but if you want help for the practice or for the Facebook Geek, the only resource I know and trust is *My Social Practice.* Jack Hadley, its founder, is a straight shooter with great ideas and systems. www.mysocialpractice.com

DENTAL INSURANCE FEE SCHEDULE RENEGOTIATION:

One of the easiest ways to increase your gross revenue is to check to make sure that your reimbursements are the most they can be. *Apex Reimbursement* can help you with that. www.apexreimbursement.com

DENTAL BILLING SERVICES:

Insurance companies are becoming stricter with their timely filing guidelines. If you want to collect all your money, consider outsourcing it. Here are two good resources.

Virtual Dental Office. www.virtualdentaloffice.net
eAssist Dental Billing. www.dentalbilling.com

DENTAL INSURANCE ALTERNATIVES:

As discussed in Chapter 43, you need to offer alternative programs to your patients. Here are two:

Plan for Health. www.planforhealth.com
Quality Dental Plan. www.qdpdentist.com

DENTAL ACCOUNTANTS:

These are two societies where you can find a CPA that specializes in dental practices:

Academy of Dental CPAs. www.adcpa.org
Institute of Dental CPAs. www.indcpa.org

DIRECT MAIL:

I believe the Madow Brothers have the best system for this, with the best results. 1-888-88MADOW. They also do excellent webinars and local seminars, and of course TBSE.

RELEASE FORMS FOR PATIENTS:

The precise language varies from state to state. If you are a client of *HR for Health*, they can provide you with the appropriate forms for both patients and employees. Otherwise I would use *LegalZoom*. www.legalzoom.com

RECEPTION TOUCHSCREEN FOR ORTHODONTISTS:

This is where you can learn more about the *Orthodontic Touchscreen* that Remarkable Dentist Kirsten Romani uses: www.orthodontictouchscreen.com

DEMOGRAPHICS AND LOCATION PLANNING:

REALscore combines world-class technology, demographics, market analysis, patient location analysis, mapping, and data to provide cutting-edge reports and consulting services to dentists and dental advisors. These resources assist in making crucial location, office, and strategic business decisions. www.realscore.com

DENTAL EMBEZZLEMENT ISSUES:

Nobody likes to think about this, but it happens a lot more than it should. David Harris with *Prosperident* knows how to detect what is occurring, and help you deal with it from a legal and practical standpoint. If you suspect your money is disappearing, or simply want to make sure you have all the appropriate controls in place, I suggest you get a hold of him. www. prosperident.com

CLAIMING YOUR PRACTICE PROFILE:

Biz.yelp.com
www.google.com/places
When you go to each of these sites, you can search for your business and claim it. They will call you on your business phone with a special code, which you use on the site to become the administrator of your profile.

PRACTICE VIDEO RESOURCES:

Magisto—this application helps you make your own fun videos from clips and photos. magisto.com

Crisp Video Group does professional quality videos for our industry and others. www.crispvideo.com

Studio Now uses a nationwide network of professional teams to cost-effectively produce great videos. www.studionow.com

UNIFORMS:

I'm a big believer in nice-looking, well-designed scrubs with your practice name on them. One place you can get some is at *Twice as Nice Uniforms.* www.twiceasniceuniforms.com

SEMINARS & TRAINING:

SIRO World is an annual meeting focused on digital dentistry, but it goes way beyond that. It has amazing inspirational speakers and breakout sessions with the latest technologies. Hosted by Sirona, it's a phenomenal opportunity to immerse yourself in the cutting edge of dentistry and be inspired for the next year. www.siroworld.com

Spear Education is the new gold standard for clinical education. Interwoven with all the excellent training from instructors headed up by Dr. Frank Spear is the wisdom and experience of Imtiaz Manji, who has helped countless dentists reach amazing performance levels. They also have some of the best clinical courses to maximize your CEREC and implant skills. www.speareducation.com

CERECdoctors.com. You'll find clinical videos here that will teach you how to handle almost any procedure that comes up. A fantastic tool for CEREC owners at every level, and you have unlimited access for a flat annual fee.

The Best Seminar Ever (TBSE) happens in Vegas every year, and it's a unique event. Put on by two dentists, Rich and Dave

Madow, the event offers an environment of fun and learning that is not to be missed. The Madows also do smaller seminars around the country throughout the year, including detailed seminars on social media and how to capitalize on it, and they are all excellent. www.madow.com and www.tbse.com

American Association of Dental Office Managers is a great organization with an annual seminar, a magazine, and continuing education that is valuable and rewarding and tailored especially for office managers. The network of members support each other all year round. Hard to beat. www.dentalmanagers.com

FRONT DESK COACHING:

Good coaching firms can certainly incorporate this, but you might also consider very specific training from one of these specialists:

TCB Dental Consulting. www.frontdesklady.com
The Gold Measure. www.thegoldmeasure.com
Miles Global. www.milesglobal.net

HYGIENE SCHEDULING AND PERFORMANCE:

Hygiene Mastery is a program that helps you build a hygiene department where extraordinary care and profitability fit together seamlessly and effectively and consistently feed the restorative and aesthetic sides of your practice.

It provides the framework for a profitable hygiene department that fully supports the total dental practice and creates a comprehensive hygiene department that provides a high level of care to your patients. www.hygienemastery.com

BOTOX AND DERMAL FILLERS TRAINING:

The most established and efficient group for this is the *American Academy of Facial Esthetics*. Founded by Dr. Louis Malcmacher, this is the most comprehensive resource for training, billing, promoting and integrating these services into your practice. www.facialesthetics.org

BLOGS AND PODCASTS:

GoAskFred. This is me, keeping you updated on everything as it happens. www.goaskfred.com

The Dental Warrior. This is Dr. Mike Barr's blog. Generally brilliant, and strong on the solo/fee-for-service approach. Do it Mike's way, and you'll be one of the few who can succeed with it as the world changes. www.dentalwarrior.com

The Thriving Dentist. Gary Takacs does amazing interviews with everyone who's anyone in dentistry. www.thrivingdentist.com

Howard Farran's podcasts. Always a high value, high entertainment experience. Find them on www.dentaltown.com

DEALING WITH
ONLINE REVIEWS

Never ignore a negative online review. Here is how you handle one:

STEP ONE: CONTACT THE PATIENT.

Email the patient directly and ask him if you can remedy the situation. You can do this as the business owner, now that you've claimed your business, even though the reviewer is anonymous. Let the patient know that you're sorry that he is displeased and if there's anything you can do, you're glad to do it. If he tells you that you can do something, by all means do it, and then ask him to please take the negative review down. (Don't ask him to do that first. Fix the problem first.)

STEP TWO: RESPOND TO THE REVIEW.

If you can't get the patient to take the review down and fix the situation yourself, now you need to respond to the negative review. And there are two things to remember here:

1. Always respond to negative reviews, but don't be defensive. Ever.
2. Use the response to essentially write an ad for your practice.

For example, the most common bad review is a patient saying that the dentist told them they needed a lot of dental work and wanted this huge amount of money—then they went to another dentist who told them that they only needed $400 of dentistry. So they think the first dentist is a crook and love the second dentist (when in reality, the first dentist presented too soon and the second dentist is afraid to present any comprehensive dentistry).

So how do you respond? The urge is to go on the defensive and insist that the patient misunderstood, the other dentist is a hack, etc. This makes you look bad and at best, accomplishes nothing. At worst, it exacerbates the situation to a war of words. Instead, respond by essentially writing an ad for your practice. Write something like this:

"We're sorry that this patient felt that way about their visit. At our practice we offer a very high standard of care and sometimes this may seem expensive at first, but we believe taking care of your teeth is very important to your general well-being and your overall health—and so we try to fully inform our patients as to their needs. We do hope this patient finds a dental practice that they love and go to regularly, because that is what's most important."

See what this does? It takes a negative situation and gives you an opportunity to say that you offer high-quality dentistry and it's too bad this person didn't want it. This makes you seem like the calm, sane person, and attracts the right patients to your practice.

STEP THREE: LET IT DIE.

Once you've responded, don't get into it anymore. If they respond back, leave it alone. You never win the war of words online.

STEP FOUR: INVITE YOUR PATIENTS TO RESPOND.

Whenever there is a negative review, the best response comes from your patients. Ask your best patients if they'd be willing to comment on the negative review, and you'll be amazed at how they will rally to your cause. And there is nothing more powerful than seeing a list of responses from patients contradicting a negative review. Viewers will see that and be extremely impressed that your own patients will rally to your defense.

A friend of mine was so embarrassed about a negative review on Yelp that he didn't want his patients to see it. I told him,

"Your best patients would be outraged to know someone was saying this about you. They will go online and rip this person to shreds. Just let them know about it, and watch what happens." Sure enough, a week later the person took the negative review down because my friend's patients pretty much humiliated the reviewer. You have patients who love you who will come to your defense, and they can say whatever they want and it doesn't put you in the middle of it.

As the business owner, you are allowed to respond to a review on Yelp and on Google. On Angie's list, people can only review you if they are a subscriber. And you can only respond if you are a subscriber, which is not that expensive, and I think worthwhile.

FOOTNOTES

1   United States Census Bureau, "2013 Highlights," http://www.census.gov/hhes/www/poverty/about/overview/

2   Futuredontics, "What Dental Patients Want," June 11, 2013

3   Futuredontics, The Changing Role of the Dental Office Manager," February 25, 2015

4   Hospital Safety Score, "Hospital Errors Are the Third Leading Cause of Death in U.S., and New Hospital Safety Scores Show Improvements Are Too Slow," October 23, 2013 http://www.hospitalsafetyscore.org/newsroom/display/hospitalerrors-thirdleading-causeofdeathinus-improvementstooslow

5   Pew Research Center, "Americans and Text Messaging," September 19, 2011

6   International Business Times, "Facebook Gets Older: Demographic Report Shows 3 Million Teens Left Social Network in 3 Years," January 16, 2014 http://www.ibtimes.com/facebook-gets-older-demographic-report-shows-3-million-teens-left-social-network-3-years-1543092

7   Salesforce, "91% of Consumers Use Email At Least Daily," September 26, 2012 http://www.exacttarget.com/blog/91-of-consumers-use-email-at-least-daily/

[8]   Futuredontics, "What Dental Patients Want," June 11, 2013

[9]   Pew Research Center, "72% of Online Adults Are Social Networking Site User," August 5, 2015 http://www.pewinternet.org/2013/08/05/72-of-online-adults-are-social-networking-site-users/

[10]   ZDNet, "Facebook accounts for 1 in every 5 page views," February 2, 2012 http://www.zdnet.com/article/facebook-accounts-for-1-in-every-5-pageviews/

[11]   Business Insider, "A Whopping 20% of Yelp Reviews Are Fake," September 25, 2013 http://www.businessinsider.com/20-percent-of-yelp-reviews-fake-2013-9#ixzz3eDB7nPNg

[12]   Harvard Health Publications, "In Praise of Gratitude," November 1, 2011 http://www.health.harvard.edu/newsletter_article/in-praise-of-gratitude

[13]   Washington Post, "Only 13 percent of people worldwide actually like going to work," October 10, 2013

[14]   DrBicuspid.com, "Study: ER visits for dental problems cost nearly $1B a year," April 2, 2015 http://www.drbicuspid.com/index.aspx?sec=sup&sub=hyg&pag=dis&ItemID=315455

[15]   The dental anywhere Blog, "Dental Anywhere Discovers the Top Ten Reasons Your Dental Office Stinks… According to Yelp Reviews," May 19, 2014 http://blog.dentalanywhere.com/top-ten-reasons-your-dental-office-stinks-according-to-yelp/#JLX4VsL5Z6wKzG72.99

[16]   Small Business Trends, "60 Percent of Online Traffic Now Comes From Mobile," July 8, 2014 http://smallbiztrends.com/2014/07/online-traffic-report-mobile.html

[17]   Business Insider, Facebook Now Serves 4 Billion Videos Per Day—Up From 3 Billion in January," April 22, 2015 http://www.businessinsider.com/facebooks-video-views-are-exploding-2015-4

[18]   Digital Sherpa," 25 Amazing Video Statistics," January, 9, 2014 http://www.digitalsherpa.com/blog/25-amazing-video-marketing-statistics/

[19]   Digital Marketing Stats, "By the Numbers: 45 Amazing Yelp Statistics," May 13, 2014 http://expandedramblings.com/index.php/yelp-statistics/

[20]   Centers for Disease Control and Prevention, " Periodontal Disease," March 10, 2015 http://www.cdc.gov/oralhealth/periodontal_disease/

[21]   Forbes, "Accounting Businesses Top List of Money-Making Industries," August 17, 2014 http://www.forbes.com/sites/sageworks/2014/08/17/ac-counting-tops-most-profitbusinesses-top-list-of-money-making-industries/